THROUGH THE EYES OF ANNIE

THROUGH THE EYES OF ANNIE

Pages Of The Past

ANGELA HART ALDRIDGE

AHARTBOOKS

I

Through The Eyes Of Annie

DEDICATION

To my beloved husband, Thomas Aldridge, This is a tribute to your profound impact on my life as a loving partner and a catalyst for discovery and connection. Through your thoughtful gesture of sharing Annie Caldwell Kennedy's diary, you opened a window into a world that has captivated my heart and soul. With immense gratitude and admiration, I dedicate these words to you, Thomas, for the incredible gift you have bestowed upon me.

With All My Love,
Your Wife

Diary of Annie Caldwell Kennedy
1874
Newspaper Clipping: At the residence of the bride's father in this
city,
June 17, 1874,
by Reverend J. Hart, Miss Annie W. Caldwell to T. L. Kennedy of

New Brighton, Beaver County, PA.

Disclaimer

This book is based on the real-life diary of my deceased relative from 1874. The diary, having been passed down through generations, was never published. It came into my possession when my boyfriend, now husband, found it in a thrift store in the mid-2000s. Through subsequent research, I discovered a familial connection to Annie Wadren Caldwell. Annie's sister's husband's parents were related to me; his mother was a Hart, which is my maiden name.

While some events and dialogues have been recreated, the essence and major events are drawn directly from the diary. Every effort has been made to preserve the original content and intent of the author. However, due to the age and condition of the diary, some modifications and interpretations may have been necessary.

It's important to note that the diary was written in 1874, and some of the language used reflects the norms and attitudes of that time, which may be considered offensive or inappropriate today. The author of this book takes no responsibility for any potential inaccuracies or omissions from the original diary. Readers should be aware that this book is a creative interpretation of historical events and should not be considered a verbatim account.

Foreword

In the following pages, we embark on a remarkable journey alongside Annie, a spirited and resilient young woman whose life unfolds gracefully and authentically. Through her vivid and heartfelt diary entries, we are transported to a bygone era, immersing ourselves in the joys, challenges, and profound moments of Annie's life in the late 19th century.

Annie's story is not just a chronicle of events but a testament to the power of love, family, and pursuing one's dreams. Within these pages, we witness Annie's growth as she navigates the complexities of relationships, embraces her sense of adventure, and faces life's trials.

Annie invites us into her world with each entry, sharing intimate glimpses of her innermost thoughts, aspirations, and reflections. From her courtship with Liv to their early years of marriage, Annie's diary provides a candid and deeply personal account of the joys and struggles of building a life together.

As we journey alongside Annie, we witness her unwavering determination to overcome adversity, whether in the face of illness, the challenges of travel, or the changes brought by time. Her resilience reminds us of the strength within each of us, inspiring us to embrace life's uncertainties and forge ahead with unwavering hope.

Through Annie's eyes, we explore the beauty of nature, the bonds of family, and the enduring power of love. We witness her connections to her childhood home, the cherished visits with relatives and friends, and the discovery of new places and experiences that shape her understanding of the world.

Annie's diary serves as a window into her life and offers us a glimpse into the broader fabric of the times. The social customs, traditions, and aspirations of 19th-century America come alive through her words, transporting us to a different era and allowing us to reflect on the progress and changes that have shaped our lives.

As we turn the pages of Annie's diary, we are reminded of preserving our stories and experiences for future generations. Annie's words bridge the past and present, linking us to the lives and legacies of those who came before us.

With great pleasure, we present this collection of Annie's diary entries—a testament to her resilience, unwavering spirit, and unwavering commitment to embracing life's journey with hope and gratitude. May her story inspire us to embrace our adventures, cherish our loved ones, and seize each day with open hearts and minds.

May we learn from Annie's wisdom, find solace in her struggles, and celebrate the triumphs of her extraordinary life. For within these pages lies a story that transcends time—a story that reminds us of the enduring power of the human spirit and the beauty of a life well-lived.

Enjoy this captivating journey through Annie's world, and may her words resonate in your hearts like mine.

Angela Hart Aldridge & Thomas Aldridge

Preface

With great pleasure and reverence, I introduce this extraordinary collection of diary entries penned by Annie, a woman whose life and experiences have left an indelible mark on the pages of history. These intimate and heartfelt reflections grant a rare glimpse into the world of a spirited and resilient individual who navigated the joys and challenges of life in the late 19th century.

Annie's diary, carefully preserved and passed down through generations, provides a remarkable window into a bygone era—a time when life moved at a different pace, and the simple pleasures held profound significance. Her words resonate with an authenticity that transcends time, allowing us to connect with her hopes, dreams, and aspirations as if they were our own.

In the following pages, we witness Annie's journey unfold—a journey of love, adventure, and personal growth. Through her eloquent prose, we traverse the landscapes of her heart, walking alongside her as she embarks on a path filled with triumphs and tribulations.

Annie's unwavering commitment to her loved ones shines through each entry, illuminating the depths of her affection and dedication. We are privy to the tender moments shared with her beloved husband, Liv, as their relationship evolves and deepens. We witness the strength of family bonds as she visits and connects with relatives, finding solace and love within the embrace of kinship.

Beyond the personal anecdotes, Annie's diary offers a glimpse into the social fabric of the time—a menagerie woven with the customs, traditions, and aspirations of 19th-century America. Through her observations, we gain insights into the ever-changing world around her, marked by progress, challenges, and the dawn of a new era.

As readers, we are invited to reflect on our journeys, drawing inspiration from Annie's resilience and determination in adversity. Her unwavering spirit reminds us that within each of us lies the power to overcome obstacles, embrace change, and find joy even in the most challenging circumstances.

It is a testament to the endurance of Annie's story that her diary has survived the passage of time and is cherished by her descendants, who recognize its profound significance. Their commitment to preserving Annie's words is a testament to the enduring power of storytelling—a means by which we connect with our past, understand our present, and shape our future.

As we embark on this literary voyage through Annie's world, let us do so with reverence, gratitude, and an open heart. May her words transport us to a different time, allowing us to reflect on the threads that bind us together as human beings, transcending the boundaries of time and space.

May we honor Annie's legacy by embracing our journeys, treasuring the connections we forge, and cherishing the moments that make life truly meaningful. For within the pages of this diary lies a testament to the beauty and resilience of the human spirit—an enduring story of love, hope, and the pursuit of a life well-lived.

With great anticipation, I invite you to immerse yourself in the world of Annie. In this world, the power of the written word serves as a bridge between generations, a testament to the enduring legacy of a remarkable woman.

Acknowledgment

Writing "Through The Eyes Of Annie- Pages of the Past": The Diary of Annie Caldwell Kennedy" has been an incredible journey filled with discovery, passion, and uncertainty. I want to take a moment to express my heartfelt gratitude to all those who have supported and contributed to the creation of this book.

First and foremost, I want to extend my most profound appreciation to Annie Caldwell Kennedy. Annie, your diary has become a treasured piece of history that has allowed me to glimpse into your life and weave this captivating tale. Your words have touched my heart and inspired me throughout this writing process.

I am also grateful to the Hart family, who married into the Caldwell family. Through extensive research, I discovered an intriguing connection to my own family on the Hart side, which happens to be my maiden last name. This unexpected and fascinating revelation has added a unique depth to my connection with Annie and her world. It's a testament to the intricate threads of our shared histories.

In particular, I would like to acknowledge Mary Isabella Caldwell, the sister of Annie Caldwell Kennedy. Mary's marriage to Frederick Oliver Dewey on the 19th day of October 1881 in Fulton County, Illinois, opened a new chapter in my family tree. Frederick Dewey's parents, Joel Wright Dewey and Louisa Hart Dewey, hold a special place in my lineage. Ironically enough, it turns out that Louisa Hart, Mary's mother-in-law, is a part of my family tree. This connection has brought a profound sense of meaning and resonance to the storytelling process.

Thank you to my family and friends for your unwavering support, encouragement, and patience. Your belief in me and this project has been a constant source of motivation. Your love and understanding during the countless hours dedicated to writing and research are deeply appreciated.

I extend my heartfelt thanks to the readers who embarked on this literary journey with me. Your curiosity, feedback, and enthusiasm fuel my passion for storytelling. I hope that Annie's story, intertwined with the lives of Mary, Frederick, Joel, Louisa, and our shared lineage, resonates with you and transports you to a bygone era.

Lastly, I want to thank all the individuals and resources that assisted me throughout my research journey. From libraries to archives, historical societies, and fellow researchers, your invaluable contributions have shed light on the past and enriched the authenticity of Annie's story.

To all those whose names I may have unintentionally omitted, please know that your support has not gone unnoticed or unappreciated. I am genuinely grateful for the collective effort that has brought "Through The Eyes Of Annie- Pages of the Past: The Diary of Annie Caldwell Kennedy" to life.

Thank you all for being a part of this extraordinary journey. May Annie's and Mary's stories inspire us to cherish our histories and embrace the "Through The Eyes Of Annie- Pages of the Past" that continue to shape our lives.

With the deepest gratitude

Chapter 1: A Victorian Wedding

June 17, 1874

Annie Caldwell stood at the threshold of a new chapter in her life. The date was June 1874, and her wedding day had finally arrived. As the sun bathed the world in its warm embrace, Annie's emotions swirled within her, a mix of excitement, nervousness, and a profound sense of anticipation. She couldn't believe that this day had finally come, the day she would join her beloved Liv in matrimony and embark on a journey that would shape their lives forever.

In her diary, Annie chronicled the flurry of activities that consumed her from the break of dawn. "For better or for worse, till death do us part. God grant it may be for better," she wrote, pouring her hopes and fears onto the page. She scarcely had a moment to sit down from the early hours of the morning until late in the afternoon. Cleaning and arranging rooms, making bouquets, cutting cakes, and setting tables left her breathless and filled with a sense of purpose. "I hardly had time to catch my breath," Annie confessed, her hands trembling with exhaustion and excitement.

The anticipation grew as the hour of the ceremony approached. "Nine P.M. was the hour set," she noted in her diary, "and we were only a few moments behind." A minor hiccup occurred when Mary K. accidentally left the lace in some unknown place, requiring a brief pause to sew it back in. The minutes she seemed to stretch, filled with both anticipation and a hint of anxiety, as Annie's heart beat faster with each passing second.

Annie's diary captured the names of their attendants, Sister Mary and Mr. Miller, who stood by their side as witnesses of their love. "Sadie Kennedy and Dan," she scribbled, the second pair of attendants. Her diary detailed their attire: the girls in white Tarleton dresses, elaborately puffed, pleated, and ruffled. Their delicate ensembles were adorned with blue flowers and sady pink, while they wore white gloves and slippers that added an elegant touch to their appearance. Annie was resplendent in a white burgundy skirt, lovingly trimmed with satin and a white satin waist. The orange blossoms she carried, along with the lovely white bouquet, were given to her by Liv's little sister, Anna, symbolizing love, purity, and new beginnings.

As the moment of departure arrived, emotions ran high. Annie's brother Lou took her in his arms as they descended the stairs. "Good-bye, Annie Caldwell, and may the dear Lord bless you," he whispered, his voice filled with pride and longing. The bittersweetness of the moment brought tears to her eyes, but she stifled them, scolding her loved ones to maintain her composure, though her heart ached at the thought of leaving them behind.

The wedding took place on the porch, officiated by Mr. Hart, as their minister, Mr. Taylor, was absent. Annie's diary captured the profound significance of the ceremony: "The moment I had dreamed of, the moment when our lives would intertwine forever, had finally arrived. The ceremony itself was a blur, as if time stood still. Yet, amidst the haze, I will always remember the exchanged vows, spoken with unwavering love and devotion, sealing our commitment in the eyes of God and our loved ones."

With the formalities concluded, the newlyweds and their jubilant guests assembled inside for a lavish supper. "Two tables were spread in the dining room," Annie reminisced in her diary. The room buzzed with laughter and conversation, a testament to the shared joy of the occasion. The company reveled in the enchanting atmosphere, savoring the delectable feast and the company of loved ones, their hearts filled with happiness and gratitude for this special day.

As the night progressed, a string band serenaded the gathering, their melodies weaving a stitch of celebration. The joyous notes filled the air, and Annie's heart was grateful. "I looked around the room, taking in the smiling faces of our friends and family," she confided in her diary. "At that moment, I realized we were not alone even though our journey might hold uncertainties. Love surrounded us, guiding us forward, and the support and well wishes of our loved ones would be our beacon in times of darkness."

Among the merriment, Annie's fears still lingered. She couldn't help but question the compatibility of their worlds. "Will we assimilate?" she pondered, her thoughts etched onto the pages of her diary. Liv had been raised in a stiff, straight-faced Eastern community, while Annie had experienced a more liberal atmosphere in the West. Doubts and wondering clouded her mind, but she knew she had to play her part in this union to bridge the gaps between their upbringings and create a harmonious life.

"As the night drew to a close," Annie confided in her diary, "Liv and I retired to our room. As we sat together, I couldn't help but feel grateful for the wonderful man I had married. Although I was still nervous about the future, I knew that together, we could face anything that came our way. We had each other's love and support; we would conquer any challenges on this shared path."

Annie's diary entries revealed the depth of her emotions, capturing her hopes, fears, and aspirations. She found solace in the pages of her diary, pouring her heart into every word. As Annie closed her diary for the night, she couldn't help but wonder what lay ahead in this new chapter of her life, ready to embrace the journey with open arms, knowing that love would guide their way.

As Annie sat in the quiet solitude of her room, her wedding gown carefully laid out on the bed, she reached for her diary again. She opened its pages with trembling hands and allowed her thoughts to flow onto the paper. 'Tonight, as I reflect on this momentous day, I am filled with a mixture of emotions,' she wrote, her pen gliding across the page with a sense of purpose and determination. 'There is joy and anticipation for the life ahead and a sense of trepidation. Will we be able to bridge the gap between our different upbringings? Can our love withstand the challenges that may come our way?' Annie's words captured the uncertainties in her heart, mingling with the flicker of hope and determination that burned within her.

As she wrote, the flickering glow of the oil lamp cast dancing shadows on the walls, adding to the room's ambiance. Outside, the stars twinkled in the vast expanse of the night sky, a silent witness to Annie's introspection. In the distance, she could hear the soft chirping of crickets and the occasional rustle of leaves in the gentle breeze, crafting a tranquil backdrop to her contemplation.

With each stroke of her pen, Annie delved deeper into her thoughts, grappling with the complexities of her new role as a wife and the uncertainties of the future. She thought of Liv, his steadfast demeanor and unwavering love giving her strength even in moments of doubt. She recalled the promises they had exchanged, vows that bound them together in a union of love and commitment.

But amidst the warmth of their shared love, Annie couldn't shake off the lingering doubts that nagged at her heart. She pondered the differences in their upbringings, the clash of cultures and expectations that threatened to sow seeds of discord in their marital bliss. She wondered if they could overcome these obstacles or if they would succumb to the pressures of societal norms and familial expectations.

As she grappled with these questions, Annie found solace in the words she penned in her diary. Each sentence was a testament to her resilience and unwavering determination to face challenges with courage and grace. She knew their love was strong enough to weather any storm, bridge the gaps between their worlds, and forge a future filled with hope and promise.

Annie closed her diary with a sense of resolve, gently pressing it against her chest as if seeking solace in the written words. In the stillness of that room, she made a silent vow to herself and Liv: to face whatever trials awaited them with courage, resilience, and unwavering love. And as she slipped into bed, the soft embrace of her wedding gown enveloping her like a cocoon, Annie felt a sense of peace wash over her. For in that moment, she knew that no matter what the future held, she and Liv would face it together, hand in hand, bound by the timeless bond of love.

Chapter 2: The Reception- A Night of Celebration

The reception hall shimmered with the soft glow of twinkling lights, casting a magical ambiance over the gathering. Annie and Liv's family and friends mingled joyously, their laughter and conversations filling the air with warmth and merriment. The room was a sight to behold, adorned with vibrant floral arrangements that added bursts of color to the elegant space. Fragrant blossoms perfumed the air, infusing the atmosphere with a delightful aroma that mirrored the couple's love and the beauty of their union.

As Annie and Liv gracefully made their way through the room, they were enveloped by smiles and well-wishes from their loved ones. Their hearts swelled with gratitude and joy, overwhelmed by the outpouring of love and support surrounding them on this particular night. The presence of their cherished friends and family reaffirmed that their union was celebrated and embraced by those closest to them, reinforcing their belief in the power of their love.

Sister Mary and Mr. Miller, Sadie Kennedy and Dan, and countless other dear friends and family members radiated happiness, their presence symbolizing the unity and support that enveloped Annie and Liv. Each heartfelt embrace and sincere congratulations only amplified their happiness, reaffirming that their union was not only a union of two souls but a joining of two families and communities.

In the joyful atmosphere, Annie's thoughts drifted to her diary, the trusted confidant where she had poured out her emotions and fears. Retrieving her diary from her room, she held it delicately in her hands, tracing her fingers over the worn pages. Her diary witnessed her deepest thoughts and desires, capturing the essence of her journey. "The reception was a whirlwind of emotions and happiness," Annie's diary entry echoed in her mind. "The love and support we received from our dear ones were overwhelming." The written words provided solace and reassurance, reminding her that her fears and uncertainties were merely transient clouds in the sky of their love.

As the evening progressed, the room continued to resonate with animated conversations and laughter. Guests savored the delicious feast, their taste buds tantalized by the carefully crafted dishes that catered to every palate. Annie was caught in a whirlwind of emotions and sensations as the room seemed to come alive with the joy and celebration of their union. Each moment etched itself into her memory, a treasured fragment of a night she would carry with her always.

But beneath the surface of her happiness, Annie couldn't escape the shadow of a doubt that lingered in her heart. Amidst the laughter and music, her mind wandered, contemplating the challenges ahead. She recognized the differences between her and Liv, merging two distinct worlds requiring understanding, compromise, and unwavering love. However, Annie remained determined to face those challenges head-on, knowing that love, understanding, and open communication would be their guiding lights.

"In the quiet solitude of my room," Annie's diary revealed, "I reflected on the evening's events." Her hand trembled slightly as she opened its pages and inscribed her thoughts: "Will our differences prove too great a challenge? Can we truly merge our separate worlds into a harmonious union?" These questions weighed heavily on her heart, but she refused to let them dampen her spirits. Love, understanding, and a willingness to embrace and appreciate their unique qualities would guide them on this journey. "With Liv by my side, I am confident that we can overcome any obstacles that may come our way," she wrote, her words laced with determination and hope.

As the night wore on, Annie found herself stealing quiet moments with Liv amidst the festivities. They shared tender glances and whispered promises of love, finding solace in each other's embrace. With each word spoken and each touch exchanged, they reaffirmed their commitment to one another, their bond growing stronger with each passing moment.

Annie and Liv found themselves drawn into the center of the festivities, their laughter mingling with the cheerful chatter of their guests. They danced together, their movements graceful and fluid, lost in the rhythm of the music and the warmth of each other's embrace. With every twirl and dip, they shared stolen moments of intimacy, their hearts beating in sync with the melody of love surrounding them.

Amid the joyous celebration, Annie stole glances at Liv, marveling at the sight of him. His eyes sparkled with happiness and adoration, his smile lighting the room with an infectious warmth. At that moment, Annie knew she was exactly where she was meant to be – in the arms of the man she loved, surrounded by their nearest and dearest, celebrating the beginning of their shared journey.

As the night wore on, the guests began to share anecdotes and well-wishes with the newlyweds, each story and sentiment adding to the fabric of love and support that enveloped Annie and Liv. Tears of joy glistened in Annie's eyes as she listened to the heartfelt words of her loved ones, grateful for the outpouring of affection that surrounded them.

Amidst the revelry, Annie's thoughts drifted to the challenges ahead. She knew their journey as husband and wife would not always be smooth sailing – there would be obstacles to overcome, disagreements to navigate, and compromises to make. But she also knew their love was strong enough to withstand any storm, their bond unbreakable in the face of adversity.

"In the quiet moments of the night," Annie whispered to Liv as they stole away to a secluded corner of the room, "I find myself wondering about the future – about the challenges we will face and the adventures we will embark on together." Her voice was soft, tinged with a hint of uncertainty, but beneath it lay an unwavering determination to conquer whatever obstacles lay ahead.

Liv took her hand in his, his touch sending a jolt of warmth through her veins. "Whatever the future holds, Annie," he said, his voice steady and reassuring, "we will face it together as partners and as equals. Our love will be our guiding light, illuminating the path ahead and giving us the strength to overcome any obstacles that may come our way."

His words were like balm to Annie's soul, soothing her fears and reaffirming her belief in their shared future. With Liv by her side, she knew they could conquer anything—together, they were unstoppable.

As the night drew to a close and the guests began to bid their farewells, Annie and Liv lingered in each other's embrace, reluctant to let go of the magic of the evening. They knew their journey as husband and wife had only begun, but as they looked into each other's eyes, they were filled with hope and anticipation for the adventures ahead.

Annie closed her diary, its pages whispering promises of hope and resilience. She placed it gently on her bedside table and let her thoughts settle as she prepared for rest. The room was bathed in the soft glow of moonlight, casting a tranquil aura over her surroundings. At that moment, Annie clung to the belief that their love was a force strong enough to conquer any uncertainties, illuminating their path toward a future filled with shared dreams and unwavering devotion.

Chapter 3: A Journey Begins

Annie Caldwell entered a new phase of her life, where the days seemed to blend in a whirlwind of change and anticipation. As she embarked on this journey, she recorded her thoughts and experiences in her diary, capturing the essence of her transformation.

"As all went to Presbyterian Church hoping to hear Mr. Bollman, but Mr. Hart preached for him," Annie's diary entry from Sabbath June 21st, 1874, echoed in her mind. She couldn't help but feel a slight disappointment as the day didn't unfold as she had expected. However, her focus quickly shifted to the afternoon visit to Yates City, where she and her loved ones shared a quiet gathering with Sister Mandy. Annie longed for a more intimate setting, wishing for Mandy to be alone so they could fully enjoy their time together. Despite the slight disappointment, the visit was a gentle reminder of the importance of cherished connections in her life.

In the aftermath of her wedding, Annie found solace and joy in the post-wedding activities. Friends and loved ones filled her home with calls and visits, creating an atmosphere of laughter and warmth. Among those who came to share her happiness were Ed Barisher from Clanton, Mr. Miller, cousin Susie Streeter, and Dame Mary. "The house is filled with calls for 'Annie' from all parts," Annie confided in her diary. "The excitement is overwhelming, but it fills my heart with joy. To see the smiles on their faces and feel their warm embraces, it's a testament to the love that surrounds me."

"The bustling excitement and laughter in the house, a reflection of the love and support that surrounded us," Annie's diary whispered, capturing her emotions. Amid the calls and visits, Annie found comfort in the familiarity of her loved ones, their presence reassuring her that she was not alone in this new chapter of her life.

But amidst the joyful chaos, Annie's attention turned to the arrival of Mr. Gray, a dear friend who had been unavoidably delayed in attending the wedding. Although unable to witness their nuptials, his presence brought comfort and familiarity to Annie's new journey. The meeting between Mr. Gray and Annie's parents held a special significance, solidifying the bonds of friendship and support that would be crucial in the coming days.

"I am grateful for Mr. Gray's visit," Annie wrote in her diary. "His kind words and reassuring presence remind me that even amid change, there are constants to hold onto. He is a reminder of the friendships that have shaped my life."

As Annie meticulously sorted through her belongings, she couldn't help but pause at certain items that held particular significance. Among them was a small, weathered journal – not her own, but one that had belonged to her mother. Opening its pages, Annie traced her fingers over the faded ink, immersing herself in the stories and reflections penned by her mother's hand. Each word was a window into her mother's world, a reminder of the legacy she had inherited. With reverence, Annie tucked the journal into her trunk, determined to carry on her mother's legacy of resilience and strength. "In her words, I find guidance and solace," Annie confided in her diary. "She may no longer be with us, but her spirit lives on in the pages of this journal."

As the days unfolded, Annie's focus shifted to the practicalities of her transition. The tasks of packing and preparing for the journey loomed before her, and she sought a delicate balance between bidding farewell to her old life and embracing the unknown. Each moment, she blended excitement and trepidation as Annie embarked on this new chapter. "I find myself torn between holding onto the familiar and stepping into the unknown," Annie mused in her diary. "Packing my belongings feels like packing away pieces of myself, memories, and stories that have shaped who I am. But there's also a sense of anticipation, a longing to discover what lies beyond."

With determination, Annie meticulously sorted through her belongings, deciding what to take and leave behind. Memories flooded her mind as she packed away trinkets and souvenirs, each holding a story and a piece of her history. She carefully folded her cherished dresses and pressed her favorite books, preparing them for the journey ahead. "I am faced with choices of what to take and leave behind," Annie reflected. "These objects may seem insignificant to others, but to me, they hold a part of my identity. They remind me of who I was and aspire to be." "The objects I hold in my hands, each with its own story and significance," Annie's diary whispered, mirroring her sentiment.

It held her hopes, fears, and aspirations within its pages, a sanctuary for her thoughts and emotions. The anticipation in the air was palpable, mirrored by the company of loved ones who accompanied Annie on a visit to Yates City. Joined by family and dear friends, they shared a heartfelt tea with Sister Mandy. In this gathering, Annie felt the powerful connection between her past and future, a bridge spanning the familiar and the unexplored. "As I sat among my loved ones, sharing stories and laughter, I felt a deep gratitude," Annie wrote in her diary. "These moments are the threads that weave the tapestry of my life. They connect me to my roots while propelling me forward into the unknown. It is a bittersweet feeling, but one filled with hope and possibility." "The conversations and laughter intertwined with a sense of gratitude and hope," Annie's diary whispered, capturing the essence of the gathering. It held the stories of that day, etching them into its pages as a testament to the connections and bonds that shaped Annie's life.

Annie reflected on the journey ahead in the days leading up to their departure. The prospect of leaving behind the familiar comforts of home filled her with excitement and apprehension. She longed for the adventures that awaited her in her new life with Liv, yet she couldn't shake the nostalgia for the life she was leaving behind. "I stand at the threshold of a new beginning, torn between the past and the future," Annie wrote in her diary. "Leaving behind the place I've always known is daunting, but I am hopeful for the adventures.

With Liv by my side, I know we can conquer whatever challenges come our way." Among the farewells, Annie was drawn to a quiet moment alone with her father. Sitting together on the porch, watching the sun set behind the rolling hills, they engaged in a conversation that stayed with Annie long after they parted ways. "I'll miss you,

Papa," Annie whispered, her voice catching with emotion. Her father embraced her warmly, his rugged hands gentle against her back. "And I'll miss you, my dear Annie," he replied, his voice tinged with sadness. "But I know that this journey is meant for you. You have a spirit of adventure, just like your mother. Embrace it, my dear, and never forget where you come from."

At that moment, Annie felt a profound gratitude for the love and wisdom her father had imparted to her. His words were a guiding light, illuminating the path ahead with warmth and reassurance. As the day of departure arrived, Annie's heart was filled with a whirlwind of emotions. She stood on the doorstep of her childhood home, her trunk packed and ready for the journey ahead. Beside her stood Liv, his hand clasped firmly in hers, a reassuring presence by her side. With tearful goodbyes and heartfelt hugs, Annie bid farewell to her family and friends; each farewells a poignant reminder of the love that surrounded her. As she stepped into the carriage beside Liv, she felt a sense of exhilaration mingled with sadness for the life she was leaving behind.

As the carriage pulled away from her childhood home, Annie cast one last glance over her shoulder, her heart heavy with the weight of goodbye. But as the landscape blurred past her window, she felt a surge of excitement for the adventures that awaited her in the arms of her beloved. With a newfound purpose and determination, Annie leaned into the journey ahead, ready to embrace whatever the future held. For in her heart, she knew the love she shared with Liv would carry them through any trials, guiding them toward their shared dreams. As the sun dipped below the horizon, casting the world in hues of gold and pink, Annie closed her eyes and allowed herself to be swept away by the promise of a new beginning.

At that moment, she knew that no matter where the road may lead, she would always find her way home – in the arms of the man she loved and in the pages of her diary, where her story would live on for generations. As Annie reflected upon these days, she marveled at the journey she had embarked upon. The path ahead was uncertain, but she faced it with bravery and vulnerability. She carried the love and support of her family, friends, and the man she had chosen to spend her life with.

Together, they would navigate the uncharted waters of marriage and create a new story—one that would be uniquely theirs. With renewed determination and purpose, Annie closed her diary, ready to embrace the challenges and adventures ahead. The journal pages held her words and the essence of her journey—a testament to her growth, resilience, and unwavering spirit. "The diary, a witness to my transformation, a testament to my journey," Annie whispered, her voice filled with anticipation. It held her hopes, fears, and dreams within its pages, capturing her essence as she stepped into the unknown.

Chapter 4: Journey Across the Lakes

Annie and Liv embarked on a remarkable journey across the lakes, their hearts brimming with excitement and anticipation. On a warm morning of June 23rd, 1874, they boarded the train for Chicago, accompanied by Mrs. Vandersloot and her daughter, Katy Rose. Their destination was Julia Wilcox's home in Donners Grove, but their path was interspersed with unexpected pauses.

They experienced a prolonged and uncomfortable wait for an accommodation train at Aurora. The time dragged on, and they sought solace in warm but tasteless soda water. The delay tested their patience, but eventually, they reached their destination, weary from the scorching heat and the humble accommodations of the half-story rooms.

"It was such a wait!" Annie's diary exclaimed. "Sadie and I were almost choked, and T.L. got us soda water, which was as warm and tasteless as suds."

During their stay in Donners Grove, Liv shared something with Annie, a revelation that stirred a mixture of sadness and a more profound trust in him. Annie's diary entry revealed her conflicting emotions: "My husband told me something, which made me feel bad but still gave me more confidence in him for his frankness. It made me realize that we are partners in this journey, capable of sharing the joys and sorrows that come our way."

The following day, they marked their departure from Donners Grove as they made their way to Chicago. Their purpose was to witness the laying of the cornerstone for the new post office, which held significant meaning for Annie. The bustling city greeted them with vibrant activity and infectious excitement. Annie's diary noted unknown words spoken during the ceremony, words that left a lasting impression on her soul.

"After the ceremony, we sought refuge at the luxurious and sophisticated Palmer House Hotel," Annie wrote in her diary. However, her health took a turn for the worse, confining her to her bed for most of the day. Despite her discomfort, Liv's kindness and attentive care provided solace amidst the missed enjoyment of the day's events.

"As evening descended, we made our way to the wharf and went aboard the steamer 'India' under the command of Captain Starkweather," Annie's diary continued. Their cozy double stateroom accommodated Noah and Sadie in one room and Annie and Liv in the other. With darkness enveloping the surroundings, they caught a glimpse of Hawkegan's distant lights to the west, bidding farewell to familiar shores.

The following morning, the vibrant city of Milwaukee welcomed them. Exploring its streets and visiting the soldiers' homes, they marveled at the city's fine architecture and warm and inviting atmosphere. The streets buzzed with the energy of its residents, and Annie found herself captivated by the diverse sights and sounds surrounding her.

Milwaukee left an indelible impression on their journey, etching fond memories in their hearts. From the friendly locals they encountered to the mouthwatering cuisine they savored, each experience added a layer of richness to their travel story. Annie's diary overflowed with vivid descriptions of the city's bustling markets, lively street performances, and the comforting aroma of freshly brewed coffee that wafted through the air.

Their voyage continued across the vast expanse of the open lake, with land becoming a rare sight. Sandy beaches punctuated the water's endless stretch, offering fleeting glimpses of the terrestrial world. On-board the steamer, they encountered a lively and pleasant company of fellow passengers. Annie highlighted twenty-one Chicago individuals bound for Batavia, New York, for a summer camping expedition. The amiable Mr. and Mrs. R. from Lowell, Massachusetts, also made their acquaintance.

"It's Funny how you meet familiar names," Annie's diary reflected. Adams and Warners among the passengers fostered a sense of camaraderie and shared experiences. We exchanged stories and laughter, creating a microcosm of friendship amidst the lake's vastness."

Familiar names aside, Annie reveled in the delights of being on the lake, with the ship's gentle rocking and breathtaking views captivating her senses. Annie and Liv found solace and joy in each other's company, cherishing intimate moments shared on the deck under the captain's watchful eye. Annie's diary revealed her profound appreciation, "Oh, it is delightful on the lake! I do enjoy it. It makes us all so sleepy rocking so. The sound of the waves lulls us into a peaceful slumber, while the vastness of the water reminds us of the infinite possibilities that lie ahead."

Mackinac offered a brief respite during their journey. In the brilliant moonlight, they explored the town, taking in the sights and even attempting to engage an old Indian in playful banter. Laughter filled the air as they experienced the magic and allure of Mackinac. The streets, aglow with the soft light of lanterns, resonated with lively music and cheerful conversations. The aroma of freshly baked pastries wafted from the local bakery, enticing their senses and drawing them closer.

Days, they were melted into one another as they traversed Lake Erie. Annie's diary shared their joy and appreciation for the beauty of nature surrounding them. She wrote, "Never can I forget the golden glory of the moon on the water and its silvery light on the land, the white walls of the houses, the mini-colored lights on the boats, and large vessels which filled the Saint Clair River. The symphony of colors and the tranquility of the scene touched a deep chord within me, reminding me of the magnificence of the natural world."

Their voyage continued, with each passing day bringing new encounters and experiences. They briefly landed in Detroit, exploring the town before rejoining their vessel. The warming weather brought relief from the bundled shawls they had relied upon for days. Singing from the Plymouth collection, their voices carried harmonious melodies across Lake Erie. The hauntingly beautiful tunes resonated with their souls, intertwining with the gentle whispers of the wind and the rhythmic lapping of the water against the ship's hull.

As Annie and Liv continued their journey across the lakes, the vastness of the waters seemed to mirror the boundless possibilities of their future together. Each passing day, they brought new adventures and encounters, weaving a collage of memories they would carry for a lifetime.

One afternoon, as the sun dipped low on the horizon, casting a golden hue across the water, Annie found herself lost in thought on the steamer's deck. Leaning against the railing, she watched the gentle sway of the waves, feeling a sense of peace settle over her.

Beside her, Liv wrapped an arm around her shoulders, drawing her close. "What are you thinking about, my love?" he asked, his voice soft and affectionate.

Annie smiled, her gaze never leaving the horizon. "I'm thinking about the journey we've been on," she replied. "About all the places we've seen and the people we've met. It's been more than I ever could have imagined."

Liv nodded, his eyes reflecting the warmth of the setting sun. "It truly has been remarkable," he agreed. "But the best part of this journey has been sharing it with you."

At that moment, Annie felt a rush of gratitude for the man beside her, for his unwavering love and companionship. Together, they faced the unknown with courage and resilience, embracing each new experience with open hearts.

As they continued their voyage, Annie found herself drawn to the stories of their fellow passengers. From the young couple embarking on their first adventure together to the elderly travelers reminiscing about journeys past, each person they encountered added a layer of richness to their story.

One evening, over a shared meal in the ship's dining room, Annie spoke with an older woman named Margaret. With twinkling eyes and a mischievous smile, Margaret regaled Annie with tales of her travels across the lakes, painting vivid pictures of days spent exploring distant shores and nights filled with laughter under the stars.

Listening to Margaret's stories, Annie felt a sense of kinship with the older woman, recognizing the shared spirit of adventure that burned within them both. As the evening wore on and the ship rocked gently beneath them, they lost themselves in conversation, trading stories and laughter late into the night.

As their journey drew close and the lights of their final destination came into view, Annie felt a bittersweet pang of sadness. Though she was eager to begin the next chapter of their adventure, she knew she would miss life's simple joys on the open water.

But as they disembarked from the steamer and set foot on solid ground again, Annie felt renewed excitement for the road ahead. With Liv by her side, she knew that no matter where their journey took them, they would face it together, hand in hand, ready to embrace whatever adventures lay in store.

So, as they bid farewell to the lakes and the countless memories they had made along their shores, Annie looked to the horizon with anticipation. She knew their journey was far from over, and the best was yet to come.

Annie's heart overflowed with gratitude for the opportunity to witness the beauty and majesty of nature on their lake journey. Every moment spent with Liv became a cherished memory, their bond growing stronger daily. In the vastness of the lakes, they discovered a profound connection to the world around them and each other, a connection that would shape their lives in ways they had yet to comprehend fully. As the days turned into weeks and their journey across the lakes continued, Annie and Liv were immersed in a kaleidoscope of experiences that enriched their souls and deepened their love.

Each sunrise brought a renewed sense of wonder as the sky was adorned with shades of gold and pink that danced upon the water's surface. Annie marveled at the beauty of the dawn, her heart swelling with gratitude for the chance to witness such breathtaking moments alongside the man she loved.

As they sailed, they encountered many fellow travelers, each with their own stories and dreams. From the pleasant campers bound for Batavia to the friendly couple from Lowell, Massachusetts, Annie and Liv found joy in the connections forged amidst the lake's vastness.

Their days were filled with laughter and conversation as they shared meals on deck and watched the ever-changing landscape unfold. They reveled in life's simple pleasures on the water, finding solace in the ship's gentle rocking and the soothing sound of the waves.

But amidst the tranquility of their journey, Annie couldn't shake the uncertainty lingering in the back of her mind. The prospect of what lay ahead weighed heavily on her heart, casting a shadow over their idyllic days on the lake.

Yet, even in uncertainty, Annie found comfort in Liv's unwavering support. His presence served as a steady source of strength and reassurance, reminding her that together, they could overcome any obstacle that came their way.

As they neared their final destination, Annie's heart swelled with anticipation for the adventures that awaited them beyond the horizon. With each passing day, her confidence in their ability to navigate the challenges of their new life grew, drawing strength from the love that bound them.

And so, as they sailed on toward the next chapter of their journey, Annie and Liv embraced the unknown with open hearts and eager spirits. For in the vastness of the lakes, they had discovered the beauty of the world around them and the depth of their love—a love that would guide them through whatever trials lay ahead.

Chapter 5: A Delightful Detour

The journey across the lakes brought Annie and Liv to Erie, where they woke up to a drudging boat cleaning the harbor. Mesmerized by the rhythmic movements and the unveiling of hidden treasures beneath the surface, Annie couldn't help but see a metaphor for life itself. "As the boat scrubbed away the dirt and grime, I pondered the moments that shape our lives, the ones that cleanse and reveal our true selves," she wrote in her diary.

After a leisurely ride through the charming town of Erie, bidding farewell to Sadie as she embarked on her adventure to Edinboro, Annie, and Liv took a leisurely walk along the shore. The wind whispered through their hair, and crashing waves filled their ears. Annie captured the moment in her diary, "In the embrace of nature's elements, I felt a sense of freedom and untamed spirit as if the wind itself carried our dreams and aspirations."

Returning to the steamer, they found themselves amidst a flurry of activity. The unloading of cargo signaled a pause in their journey, and Annie couldn't help but marvel at the synchronicity of it all. "Just as the boat shed its burdens, I too felt a weight lifted from my shoulders," she penned. The boat's rocking in the strong wind added an exhilarating touch to their voyage, reminding Annie of the delicate balance between stability and adventure.

As they set foot on the dry dock in Buffalo, Annie felt a surge of excitement mingled with a hint of nostalgia. The city's historic charm beckoned them to explore its hidden corners. Their encounters with Miss Garlinghouse, a teacher from Peoria who knew familiar names from their journey, added a lucky touch to their day. Annie mused, "In the assortment of connections, I marveled at how our paths intertwine, weaving stories and memories that transcend time."

Seeking respite and rejuvenation, they found themselves at the mansion house, a grand reminder of a bygone era. The luxury of the surroundings stirred Annie's imagination, and she imagined the stories of love, triumph, and dreams that the walls whispered. "In the embrace of history's embrace, I found solace and inspiration, knowing that our own story is but a chapter in the larger life narrative," she confided in her diary.

Guided by Captain Starkweather and the Simon family, Annie and Liv embarked on a journey through the streets of Buffalo. Laughter filled the air as they shared a delightful dinner, the camaraderie forging new bonds of friendship. Annie's heart swelled with gratitude for the moments of connection, and she immortalized the evening in her diary, "In the company of kindred spirits, we ventured through the city's streets, our laughter intertwining with the echoes of those who came before us."

Their wanderings led them to the house where Mr. and Mrs. Alfred Gray had begun their married life—a place fondly called "a little paradise." Annie found herself captivated by Buffalo's beauty, her senses heightened by the splendor of Delaware Street. "Delaware Street, a living canvas of architectural marvels, painted a picture of the possibilities within our grasp," she marveled.

The delay caused by a freight mishap on their journey to Niagara only heightened their anticipation. The moonlit rapids cast a spell on Annie as they lay on the road, their patience rewarded with a glimpse of nature's enchantment. "In the hushed moments of waiting, the rapids whispered tales of ancient power, reminding me of the vastness and beauty of the world," she wrote.

Finally, the hour arrived, and they reached Niagara, weary but filled with wonder. The Cataract House stood before them, a haven amidst the natural wonder surrounding them. From the porch, Annie gazed upon the illuminated rapids, their dance of light and sound captivating her soul. "The rapids, a symphony of nature's artistry, invited me to surrender to their timeless rhythm," she confided.

With the dawn of a new day, Annie and Liv rose, their weariness replaced by excitement for the adventures awaiting them. They indulged in a leisurely breakfast, savoring each bite as a symbol of nourishment and renewal. The carriage ride to Goat Island and Luna unveiled new dimensions of Niagara's splendor, igniting a sense of childlike wonder within Annie. She described the experience in her diary as "a dance with nature's majesty, where every step brought us closer to the heart of the falls."

Annie eagerly donned the oil-cloth suit and embarked on the 164-step journey to the Cave of the Winds. With each step, she felt the misty spray of the falls on her face, a reminder of her resilience in facing life's challenges. "In the embrace of the falls' power, I discovered the strength within me, a strength that could weather any storm," she wrote.

Their exploration continued as they visited Three Sisters Island and crossed to the Canadian side, marveling at the falls from a different perspective. The park beckoned them with its lush greenery and scenic views while the inclined plane offered a thrilling ascent. A leisurely dinner allowed Annie to savor the region's flavors, intertwining with the forged memories. As they strolled through town before departing for Buffalo, Annie's heart swelled with gratitude for the unfolding beauty and experiences.

The journey across the lakes and their arrival in New Brighton had become more than a physical voyage. It was a testament to the power of discovery, connection, and self-transformation. Annie marveled at how each destination had woven itself into the fabric of her being, enriching her journey through life.

As Annie and Liv prepared to embark on the next chapter of their adventure, she held onto the cherished moments in her heart, knowing that they would forever serve as a guiding light. The journey across the lakes had brought them closer to the depths of their souls, revealing the possibilities ahead. And with that understanding, they stepped forward into the unknown, ready to embrace whatever the future held.

Their journey across the lakes had been more than just a physical voyage; it was a transformative odyssey that etched itself into the very core of their beings. As they bid farewell to the majestic Niagara Falls, Annie and Liv expressed profound gratitude for the unfolding experiences, each moment leaving an indelible mark on their souls.

With their hearts still reverberating with the echoes of nature's splendor, Annie and Liv resumed their journey with renewed purpose and anticipation. Their next destination beckoned from afar, promising new adventures and discoveries that awaited them on the horizon.

As they journeyed onward, the landscape gradually shifted around them, revealing new vistas and landscapes that captured their imagination. The quaint towns and bustling cities they encountered along the way offered glimpses into the region's rich mosaic of life, each presenting its unique charm and allure.

In the bustling port city of Cleveland, Annie and Liv were captivated by the vibrant energy that permeated the streets. The bustling markets and lively waterfront offered a feast for the senses, while the historic landmarks and architectural marvels stood as testaments to the city's storied past.

While exploring the city's hidden gems, Annie and Liv stumbled upon a quaint café in a cobblestone alley. There, amidst the aroma of freshly brewed coffee and the soothing melodies of live music, they found solace and companionship in each other's company. Moments like these, simple yet profound, it reminded them of the beauty of shared experiences and the joy of being together.

As they continued their journey, Annie and Liv were drawn to the tranquil beauty of the Great Lakes, where the vast expanse of water stretched out before them in all its majesty. The soft lapping of the waves against the shore and the distant call of seagulls created a sense of serenity that enveloped them like a warm embrace.

In the quiet moments spent gazing out across the endless horizon, Annie and Liv contemplated the mysteries of life and the boundless possibilities that lay ahead. It was a time of reflection and introspection, a chance to connect with the deeper truths that resided within their souls.

As they traversed the lakes, Annie and Liv encountered a diverse array of fellow travelers, each one with their own stories and aspirations. From seasoned sailors to adventurous explorers, they were immersed in a community of kindred spirits, bound together by a shared love for adventure and discovery.

Amidst the laughter and camaraderie shared with their fellow travelers, Annie and Liv forged new friendships that would last a lifetime. Together, they reveled in the joys of exploration and the thrill of experiencing the unknown, finding solace and companionship in the company of like-minded souls.

As they sailed onward, the horizon stretched like an empty canvas, awaiting the colors of their dreams and aspirations. With each passing mile, Annie and Liv felt their spirits soar with excitement for the adventures that lay ahead, knowing that together, they could conquer any challenge that came their way.

And so, with hearts full of hope and anticipation, Annie and Liv embraced the journey before them, ready to chart a course into the unknown and write the next chapter of their extraordinary adventure across the lakes.

Chapter 6: Summer Surprises

The sun beat down relentlessly on the Fourth of July, casting a golden hue over the quaint town of New Brighton. Annie welcomed the absence of demonstrations, knowing that the heat would have made the festivities less enjoyable. Instead, she found solace in Liv's spontaneous idea to embark on a delightful ride to Beaver early in the morning, offering a refreshing escape from the sweltering weather.

As they journeyed through the picturesque countryside, Annie couldn't help but marvel at the beauty surrounding them. Each rolling hill and verdant meadow seemed to whisper secrets of tranquility and serenity, urging her to savor the moment. She longed to etch the scenery into her memory, preserving it as a testament to the simple joys of life.

Upon arriving in Beaver, Annie and Liv invited Annie's cousin, Miss Mary McGaffick, to join them for their summer adventures in New Brighton. Mary's addition infused their days with newfound camaraderie and companionship, enriching their shared experiences.

"The ride to Beaver was delightful," Annie penned in her diary. "The landscape was so picturesque, I wish I could etch its beauty into my memory forever."

Despite the oppressive heat, they made the most of their time indoors, engaging in leisurely activities and heartfelt conversations. However, as the evening approached, Sam Miller arrived with a carriage, offering them a chance to escape the confines of the stifling air. Together, they embarked on a leisurely ride, visiting a charming picture gallery adorned with exquisite transparent views that captivated their senses.

"Sam Miller came with a carriage, and we took a ride," Annie recorded in her diary. "The picture gallery was a delightful escape from the summer heat, its vibrant colors bringing joy to our hearts."

Their excursion continued as they ventured to a quaint restaurant, where they indulged in delectable treats and shared lighthearted conversations. Laughter filled the air, mingling with the sweet aroma of freshly baked pastries, creating a medley of cherished memories that Annie held close to her heart.

"In the evening, we went to a restaurant and enjoyed delicious treats," Annie reminisced in her diary. "The laughter and joyful conversations were a balm to our souls, weaving bonds of friendship that would endure."

In the days that followed, Annie was swept up in a whirlwind of events, each moment fleeting yet significant. One particular highlight was the visit of Liv's close friend, Harvey McGrury, and his wife, accompanied by Miss Lou Wilson. Their presence brought a sense of warmth and familiarity to their summer days, infusing each gathering with laughter and camaraderie.

"Harvey McGrury and his wife visited us," Annie noted in her diary. "Their friendship brought joy and a sense of belonging to our summer days."

Amidst the festivities, Annie was invited to a reception in their honor, a grand affair that filled her heart with pride and gratitude. Donning her wedding dress adorned with delicate blue flowers, she mingled with the guests, basking in the warmth of their friendship and the beauty of the occasion.

"I wore my wedding dress with blue flowers and a sash," Annie recalled fondly in her diary. "The reception was a grand affair, a testament to the bonds of friendship we had forged in our new community."

Soon after, Annie embarked on a journey to Pittsburgh to visit her dear friend, Annie McClelland, who was about to embark on an exciting journey of her own. Annie cherished the opportunity to reconnect with her friend and explore the bustling city, all while relishing the company of loved ones.

I visited my friend Annie McClelland in Pittsburgh," Annie wrote in her diary. She is about to embark on an incredible journey, and I couldn't be happier for her."

Meanwhile, Liv encountered unexpected challenges during his visit to Allegheny, where he had planned to meet Uncle Andrew at the market. Hindered by unforeseen circumstances, he found himself wandering the unfamiliar streets late into the night, his determination guiding him through the darkness until he finally reached his destination.

"Liv had a challenging time reaching Uncle Andrew's place," Annie recorded in her diary. "I was relieved when he finally arrived, tired but safe."

Despite their trials, Annie and Liv remained steadfast in their resolve to embrace each new adventure with open hearts and unwavering determination. With their sights set on Mercer County, they eagerly anticipated the surprises and delights that awaited them, ready to embrace whatever the future held.

"Excitement fills the air as we embark on a new adventure," Annie reflected in her diary. "Together, we will navigate the unknown, hand in hand, and emerge stronger and more resilient than ever."

As they journeyed through the scenic countryside, Annie was lost in thought, reflecting on their adventures in New Brighton. The memories of their Fourth of July escapade and the warmth of the community lingered in her mind, filling her with a sense of gratitude for their experiences.

As they passed through familiar landscapes, Annie couldn't help but notice the subtle changes that marked the transition from one town to the next. Each quaint village they encountered had its own story to tell, its history woven into the fabric of the land. Liv pointed out landmarks along the way, sharing anecdotes from his travels and adventures.

Their journey took them through rolling hills and verdant meadows, the landscape unfolding like a painting before their eyes. Annie breathed in the fresh country air, feeling a sense of peace wash over her as they traveled farther from the bustling town of New Brighton. It was a welcome respite from the noise and chaos of everyday life, a chance to reconnect with nature and each other.

As they drove on, Annie and Liv engaged in lighthearted banter and shared laughter, their spirits lifted by the beauty of their surroundings. They stopped for a picnic by a babbling brook, spreading out a blanket beneath the shade of a towering oak tree. Annie marveled at the simplicity of the moment, savoring each bite of their homemade sandwiches and reveling in the company of her beloved husband.

As the afternoon sun descended toward the horizon, they resumed their journey, the soft golden light casting a warm glow over the countryside. Annie leaned back in her seat, content to watch the world pass by outside the window. She felt a sense of peace settle over her, knowing she was precisely where she was meant to be, with the person she loved most by her side.

As evening approached, they arrived back in New Brighton, the familiar sights and sounds of home welcoming them back with open arms. Annie felt a sense of comfort wash over her as they pulled into their driveway, the warmth of their cozy little house enveloping her like a familiar embrace.

As they unpacked their belongings and settled back into their routine, Annie couldn't help but feel grateful for their shared journey. Though they had only been briefly away, their adventures had left an indelible mark on her heart, reminding her of the beauty and wonder that could be found in the simplest moments.

With a smile and a heart full of love, Annie knew that no matter where their journey took them next, she would always treasure the memories they had created together in New Brighton. As they settled in for the night, she drifted off to sleep with a sense of contentment, knowing she was precisely where she was meant to be.

Chapter 7: Treasured Memories

The day before their anticipated journey on August 10th, 1875, Annie and Liv decided to visit Mount Senickley Camp Meeting, immersing themselves in the serenity and spiritual atmosphere of the grounds. Annie's diary entry described the setting as lovely, with picturesque surroundings that embraced them in tranquility. The couple found solace and peace amidst the natural beauty that enveloped them, creating a cherished memory in Annie's heart.

"Our visit to Mount Senickley Camp Meeting was simply lovely," Annie wrote in her diary. "The serene atmosphere and picturesque surroundings enveloped us in tranquility."

After their soulful visit to the camp meeting, Annie and Liv continued their adventure, going to Pittsburgh. It was there that Liv surprised Annie with a special gift—an exquisite set of silverware. Annie vividly recalled the details in her diary, mentioning the silver knives, solid forks, three solid tables, and three dessert spoons, all perfectly matching. This thoughtful gesture symbolized their love and commitment to each other, becoming a cherished memento of their journey together.

"Liv surprised me with a set of silverware," Annie joyfully noted in her diary. "The silver knives, solid forks, and dessert spoons are exquisitely matched—a symbol of our love and commitment."

Their journey led them to Mercer County, where they embarked on a grand round of visits to various relatives. The names of McCormick's, Wilson's, and Walkers resonated in Annie's diary as they visited Sharon, immersing themselves in the warmth and love of family connections. Their curiosity took them even further to the town of Sharpsville, where they marveled at the magnificence of the Pierce mansion. With a staggering value of $150,000, it stood as the grandest house Annie had ever laid eyes on, leaving an indelible impression on her.

"In Mercer County, we made a grand round of visits," Annie recalled in her diary. "We visited Sharon and were immersed in the warmth and love of our family. We also saw the awe-inspiring Pierce mansion in Sharpsville, which left me in awe."

The exploration continued as they traveled to Transfer, where they visited Uncle Thompson, Uncle Daniel Livingston, and Aunt Mary Livingston in Clarksville. Each visit strengthened family bonds, shared stories, and created lasting memories. From there, they journeyed to Uncle Samuel Caldwell's residence, followed by a visit to Mercer and Uncle Hamilton's. Annie delighted in the rhythm of their travels, experiencing the unique beauty of each place and savoring the moments that would forever remain etched in her heart.

"One of our cherished excursions took us to Stoneboro," Annie reminisced in her diary. "We embarked on a pleasure excursion to Sandy Lake, a lovely piece of water adorned with delicate lilies. We spent a blissful half-day reveling in the beauty of nature."

Amidst the joyous exploration, Liv received a letter calling him back home, interrupting their blissful adventures. Annie visited each place more, cherishing the moments spent with family and friends. She visited Uncle George Menolds and Greenville, visiting Franks and Mrs. Bittenbanners. These connections were precious to her, and she cherished the warmth and love that radiated from every encounter.

As Liv and Annie's paths again intertwined, they reunited at Transfer before journeying to Sharon. There, they spent a sacred Sabbath, embracing the serenity of the day and finding comfort in each other's presence. However, the time came for Liv to leave Annie there, promising to return by the end of the week.

Annie continued her journey, making her way back home. Along the way, she made another visit to Salem, finding solace in the treatment offered by Lady Physician Miss Lizzie Grisele. These visits became a source of support and healing for Annie, giving her the strength to face each new day.

"With each visit to Salem, I found solace and support," Annie reflected in her diary. "The treatment offered by Miss Lizzie Grisele brought me much-needed relief."

As the seasons changed, Annie made several trips to Salem, savoring the fall drives and feeling the positive impact of the treatment. The last visit of the year occurred on December 10th, marking the end of a chapter filled with personal growth, familial connections, and the pursuit of well-being.

Annie's spirit grew stronger with each passing day, fueled by the love and support she received from her family and friends and the memories they had created together. She embraced life's joys and challenges, determined to make the most of every moment.

The journeys Annie undertook were physical explorations and opportunities for inner transformation. Through her encounters with different places and people, she discovered new facets of herself and gained a deeper understanding of the world around her. She learned to appreciate the simple pleasures, finding beauty in the most minor details and solace in nature's embrace.

"With gratitude in my heart, I embrace the lessons and memories of the past," Annie reflected. "Equipped with these experiences, I am ready to navigate the twists and turns of life's journey."

As Annie turned the page to a new chapter, she was hopeful. She knew that life would continue to unfold, bringing joyous moments and unforeseen obstacles. However, armed with the memories and lessons of the past, she was ready to embrace whatever lay ahead, confident in her ability to navigate the patchwork of life.

With renewed determination, Annie embarked on the next phase of her journey, eager to see what the future held. She bid farewell to the familiar landscapes and faces, carrying the cherished memories in her heart. The roads stretched before her, inviting her to new destinations, experiences, and revelations.

Annie's travels led her to new towns and cities, each with its own distinct charm and character. She marveled at the majestic Lawrence County Courthouse in New Castle, symbolizing justice and community. The bustling streets and vibrant markets of Beaver Falls captivated her senses, offering a glimpse into the everyday lives of the people who called it home.

As she ventured further, Annie found herself in Washington,

Pennsylvania, a town steeped in history and tradition. She explored the quaint shops and admired the stately Victorian architecture adorned the streets. In the local library, she lost herself in the pages of books, finding solace and inspiration in the written word.

Annie's journey also took her to the charming town of Waynesburg, nestled amidst the rolling hills of Greene County. The peacefulness of the countryside enveloped her, and she took long walks, basking in the beauty of nature. The vibrant colors of autumn painted a breathtaking picture, reminding her of the ever-changing cycles of life.

In Uniontown, Annie discovered the beauty of Friendship Hill, a historic estate overlooking the majestic Monongahela River. The sprawling gardens and meticulously preserved house spoke of a bygone era, inviting her to imagine the lives of those who had walked its halls. She marveled at the stories etched into the walls and pondered the legacy she would leave behind.

Annie's journey was about the places and people she encountered. Each interaction left an indelible mark on her soul, reminding her of the power of human connection. From the friendly shopkeepers who shared stories of their town's history to the fellow travelers who exchanged tales of their adventures, Annie found inspiration and camaraderie in the shared experiences of others.

As the year drew close, Annie reflected on the chapters she had written in her diary. Each page held a piece of her journey, a fragment of her growth. The challenges she faced, the moments of joy, and the lessons learned were all woven together to form the montage of her life.

With the new year on the horizon, Annie felt a renewed sense of purpose and a deep gratitude for the experiences that had shaped her. She knew the road ahead would be filled with twists and turns, but she embraced it wholeheartedly. Armed with the memories and wisdom she had gained, she was ready to face whatever lay ahead.

As Annie closed the chapter on her travels and prepared to write the next, she carried the lessons learned, the connections made, and the beauty discovered. She entered the unknown with her diary, eager to continue weaving the intricate threads of her life's story. As she turned each page, she knew that the unfolding tale was uniquely hers—a testament to her resilience, spirit, and unwavering belief in the power of a journey well-traveled.

Chapter 8: Embracing New Beginnings

As December enveloped New Brighton in a frosty embrace, Annie and her family settled into their new home, a testament to Father Kennedy's perseverance and hard work. The house's spacious rooms and cozy corners provided a welcome respite from the winter chill, offering a sanctuary where cherished memories could take root and flourish.

"In December, Father Kennedy's new house was finally completed, and we moved from Fallston to New Brighton," Annie wrote in her diary. "Although we had planned to start our household in the fall, objections from Mother K. and others forced us to postpone our plans. The new house is large and roomy, and I particularly love the spacious northwest room with its pleasant view of the factory, dam, and bustling street."

Cousin Liv Caldwell's visit further amplified the joy of their new home. Liv surprised Annie with thoughtful gifts to celebrate the occasion—a stand work-basket, a cozy hassock, and various other items. The rest of the family also showered her with small tokens of affection, while Cousin John Caldwell presented her with a beautiful carving set. Overwhelmed with gratitude, Annie marveled at the love and generosity that surrounded her.

As the calendar turned to January 1875, Annie's dear friend, Annie McClelland, visited her. Their days were filled with laughter, shared memories, and heartfelt conversations, reaffirming the strength of their enduring friendship. The reunion of kindred spirits brought joy to Annie's heart immeasurable, and she cherished every moment they spent together.

In the following month of February, Annie's health took a severe blow when she experienced a prolonged and painful bout of quinsy. The illness persisted for two weeks, leaving her weak and drained as spring approached. To compound matters, her previous health issues resurfaced, reminding her of the challenges she had faced even before her marriage.

After consulting with Dr. Giselle, it was decided that Annie should seek treatment at her location. With great determination, she embarked on a journey in early May, hoping to find relief and healing. Under Dr. Giselle's care, Annie endured various treatments targeting her eyes, throat, and other affected areas. The process was arduous, and she experienced moments of significant discomfort. However, she found solace in knowing these efforts were crucial for her well-being. Gradually, the treatment proved beneficial, restoring her strength and instilling a renewed sense of hope.

Upon returning home, Annie's spirits were lifted, and she felt a new-found vitality coursing through her veins. She had endured hardships and tribulations, emerging on the other side with a sense of resilience. As their anniversary approached, Annie had a photograph taken of herself in her wedding clothes, a heartfelt gift for Liv. In return, Liv surprised her with a lovely ring adorned with a coral medallion, sym-bolizing his enduring love and devotion.

In preparation for an upcoming visit to Annie's hometown, the couple made a brief trip to Pittsburgh to gather necessary supplies and make arrangements. Annie was thrilled to have Annie McClelland accompany her on this journey, cherishing the opportunity to share cherished memories and experiences with her dear friend.

In the weeks before their journey, Annie and Liv busied them-selves with preparations, ensuring they had everything they needed. Liv meticulously packed their belongings while Annie took care of the last-minute details, ensuring they wouldn't forget anything important. Their excitement bubbled over as they made their final arrangements. Annie couldn't wait to introduce Liv to her family and show him all the places she held dear from her childhood. The thought of revisiting familiar haunts with her beloved husband filled her with a warmth that spread from her heart to her fingertips.

Their journey commenced as they boarded the train bound for Annie's hometown. Annie couldn't suppress the smile on her lips as the rhythmic chug of the locomotive and the gentle sway of the carriage added to her sense of anticipation, heightening the thrill of the journey ahead. Throughout the trip, Annie and Liv shared stories and dreams, weaving their hopes for the future into the accumulation of their shared memories. They spoke of building a life together, the adventures they would embark upon, and the family they hoped to create one day.

Annie's heart swelled with nostalgia and excitement as the train chugged closer to their destination. She couldn't wait to step off the train and feel the familiar embrace of her hometown once more. It had been too long since she last walked its streets, and she relished the thought of rediscovering the magic of her youth with Liv by her side. As the train pulled into the station, Annie's pulse quickened with anticipation. The journey ahead was not merely a physical one but a journey of the heart—a return to her roots, where her story began. And with Liv by her side, she knew this homecoming would start a new chapter in their lives—a chapter filled with love, laughter, and the promise of tomorrow.

Upon their return from Pittsburgh, the family eagerly prepared for the highly anticipated Alumni Reception in Beaver, organized by Mrs. McGriery. The event was a momentous occasion in the small town, drawing together former students and acquaintances and creating an atmosphere of warmth and nostalgia. Annie felt excited as she carefully chose her attire for the evening, opting to wear her lavender silk gown for the first time.

A wave of mixed emotions washed over Annie as she adorned herself in her party finery. She couldn't help but acknowledge that such extravagances seemed out of place in the quiet town of New Brighton, where social gatherings were few and far between. In a place where simplicity was cherished, and the pace of life was unhurried, she questioned whether her lavish attire might seem ostentatious to the locals. However, she also recognized the importance of embracing the moments of celebration life offered, and she honored the occasion by donning her finest attire.

As Annie stepped into the Alumni Reception, she was greeted by familiar faces and warm embraces. The room buzzed with conversations, laughter, and the joy of reconnecting with old friends. It was a testament to the power of community and the lasting impact of shared experiences. Annie's heart swelled with gratitude for the bonds she had formed throughout her life, both in her hometown and her new surroundings. Amid the lively atmosphere, Annie found solace in knowing that true fulfillment did not solely reside in grand events and extravagant gatherings.

She had learned to adapt and find contentment in the simplicity of her surroundings, cherishing the day-to-day moments and the love shared with her family and friends. Through these connections, she discovered a profound sense of fulfillment and purpose. Each passing day, she brought new opportunities for growth and joy. Annie embraced the present, finding beauty in the ordinary moments of her life—the laughter shared with loved ones, the comforting conversations, and the quiet reflections. She had come to understand that life's journey was intriguing, woven with grand adventures and peaceful moments of introspection.

With renewed optimism, Annie looked toward the horizon, eager to set out on new adventures and welcome the opportunities ahead. She knew life was an ever-changing and unpredictable journey but faced it with resilience and an open heart. As she closed the chapter on this phase of her life, Annie carried with her the lessons learned, the cherished memories, and the enduring friendships that would continue to shape her story. And so, in the face of new beginnings and the familiarity of cherished relationships, Annie stepped forward with a sense of gratitude and anticipation. She embraced the ebb and flow of life's journey, knowing that despite the simplicity and complexity, something beautiful was always to be discovered.

Chapter 9: A Homecoming

July 2nd, 1875: Started the journey home today with Cousin Susie Menold. It felt good to be on the road, but I couldn't help missing my dear husband, Liv. It's strange how marriage can create a divide between lifelong friends, occupying a unique place in one's life.

During our journey, we embarked on a tour of Mercer County. It had been nine long years since my last visit, and the anticipation filled my heart. We first stopped in Galesburg, where we visited Mr. Stewart's. The memories flooded back, and I couldn't help but feel a sense of nostalgia and warmth. From there, we continued our journey, visiting Susie Strielers, Barbara Parks, Will Menolds, and Mrs. Beechlers. Each visit was a testament to the bonds that shaped my life and the enduring connections formed over the years. Our journey took us to Uncle Stewart Caldwell's at North Henderson before we returned home via Monmouth and Galesburg. The visits left an indelible mark on my heart, reinforcing the significance of the relationships that have been a part of my journey.

While at home, I cherished the company of Mandie and Lou, spending weeks with each of them. However, the thought of my dear friend Libbie moving to Stuart, Iowa, weighed heavily on my mind. The uncertainty of our paths crossing again cast a shadow of melancholy, reminding me of the transient nature of life and the inevitable changes that lie ahead.

A visit from Mary R. and Elsie brought joy to my homecoming. We engaged in various activities and even created beautiful wax crosses together. I carefully packed my cross, intending to return it to Pennsylvania as a cherished memento—a reminder of the bonds forged during my time at home. However, our joy was tempered when Mary R. faced a health complication. Seeking treatment in Galesburg, she returned home sooner than expected, suffering from a painful abscess under her arm. We rallied around her, offering comfort and support during her recovery, reaffirming the strength of our bond and the importance of standing together in times of adversity.

As I prepared for my future household, my mother gifted me 125 yards of exquisite rag carpet for the dining room and kitchen. It was a tangible symbol of her love and support, a reminder that I am not alone in this new chapter of my life. Together, we packed my belongings and carefully stored the numerous sentimental items I had received during my time at home. Each item held memories and meaning, a testament to the connections forged and the experiences that have shaped me. Boxes and barrels were filled, ready to accompany me on the journey back, marking a significant step toward the next phase of our lives together.

With the preparations complete and memories of home and loved ones firmly etched in my heart, I eagerly anticipate the next chapter of my journey. The experiences and connections formed during my time at home will serve as a foundation for the adventures and challenges ahead, empowering me to embrace the future with hope and resilience. Little do I know that the journey I have just embarked upon is merely the beginning—a prelude to a tale of love, growth, and the pursuit of a life filled with purpose and fulfillment. I am captivated by the twists and turns that await me, eager to discover what lies beyond the horizon.

Excitement and trepidation filled my being as bidding farewell to the familiar comforts of home. The path before me is unknown, yet a deep curiosity and a yearning for new experiences fuels me. The road stretches like an unwritten story, beckoning me to embrace its challenges and revelations.

Each step reminds me of the countless individuals who have shaped my journey thus far. Their words of encouragement and unwavering support echo in my mind, giving me the strength to face whatever lies ahead. The lessons learned from loved ones and kindred spirits will be my guiding light as I navigate the uncharted territories of life.

Along this path, I know I will encounter obstacles and setbacks. The road may become rugged, and uncertainty may weigh heavily on me. But I am determined to persevere, to draw upon my resilience, and to transform challenges into opportunities for growth. It is through adversity that true strength is forged, and I am prepared to rise to the occasion.

As I venture into the vast expanse of the world, I am humbled by its immensity. Countless cultures, traditions, and perspectives await me, ready to broaden my understanding of the human experience. Each encounter will be an opportunity for connection, having a chance to learn and appreciate the diversity that enriches our collective blend.

The excitement and unknown, I carry with me the values instilled by my upbringing—a strong sense of integrity, compassion, and a belief in the power of kindness. These virtues will be my compass, guiding my actions and interactions with others. I am resolved to leave a positive imprint on the lives I touch, uplift, and inspire, even in the most minor ways.

As the scenery changes around me, I am reminded of the ever-changing nature of life itself. Seasons come and go, and with them, the ebb and flow of joys and sorrows. I embrace this impermanence, knowing that it is through the constant evolution of self that actual growth is nurtured.

With an open heart and an adventurous spirit, I embark on this journey that promises to unravel the depths of my soul and challenge my perceptions. I am ready to learn, adapt, and embrace the unknown with wonder and curiosity. Whatever the future may hold, I am confident it will shape me into the person I am meant to become.

And so, as I take my first steps into the vast unknown, I carry the memories of home and loved ones with me. Though physically distant, their presence will forever reside within my heart, offering solace and encouragement. With gratitude for the chapters that have already been written, I eagerly turn the page, ready to pen the next chapter of my remarkable journey.

The lessons learned from loved ones and kindred spirits will be my guiding light as I navigate the uncharted territories of life. Along this path, I know I will encounter obstacles and setbacks. The road may become rugged, and uncertainty may bear heavily upon me. However, I am determined to persevere, draw upon my resilience, and transform challenges into opportunities for growth. It is through adversity that true strength is forged, and I am prepared to rise to the occasion.

As I venture into the vast expanse of the world, I am humbled by its immensity. Countless cultures, traditions, and perspectives await me, ready to broaden my understanding of the human experience. Each encounter will be an opportunity for connection, a chance to learn and appreciate the diversity that enriches our collective blend.

The excitement and unknown, I carry with me the values instilled by my upbringing—a strong sense of integrity, compassion, and a belief in the power of kindness. These virtues will be my compass, guiding my actions and interactions with others. I am resolved to leave a positive imprint on the lives I touch, uplift, and inspire, even in the most minor ways.

As the scenery changes around me, I am reminded of the ever-changing nature of life itself. Seasons come and go, and with them, the ebb and flow of joys and sorrows. I embrace this impermanence, knowing that it is through the constant evolution of self that actual growth is nurtured.

With an open heart and an adventurous spirit, I embark on this journey that promises to unravel the depths of my soul and challenge my perceptions. I am ready to learn, adapt, and embrace the unknown with wonder and curiosity. Whatever the future may hold, I am confident it will shape me into the person I am meant to become.

And so, as I take my first steps into the vast unknown, I carry the memories of home and loved ones with me. Though physically distant, their presence will forever reside within my heart, offering solace and encouragement. With gratitude for the chapters that have already been written, I eagerly turn the page, ready to pen the next chapter of my remarkable journey.

Chapter 10: Reunion and Rainy Travels

On September 4th, 1875, a momentous journey began as Annie and her sister Mary set off for Pennsylvania, excitedly and excited. They bid farewell to their family and familiar surroundings, leaving their hometown behind. They found respite at Mr. Stewart's residence in Galesburg, which was warmly welcomed and offered a temporary sanctuary. Annie's diary entry captured their arrival in Chicago during a heavy rainstorm. Despite the downpour, they persevered and went to Alice George's residence on West Harrison Street. Upon reaching their destination, Annie noted their bedraggled state, where they received hospitality and kindness from Alice. She took care of their soiled skirts, washing, drying, and pressing them, for which Annie expressed gratitude.

Refreshed and grateful, the sisters explored the city with Mrs. George as their guide. Annie's diary recounted their tour of Chicago, visiting Lincoln Park and other places, immersing themselves in the vibrant streets and iconic landmarks. The Exposition impressed Annie, particularly the "Eastlake" style rooms she found unique and pretty. Their journey continued aboard the Michigan Southern and Lake Shore Railroad, but an error led them onto a northern branch, causing a delay in reaching Cleveland. Annie lamented the situation in her diary as they arrived in the city at 3 P.M., much later than expected.

Despite setbacks, Annie and Mary remained determined, fueled by a delightful breakfast in Adrian, Michigan. The flavors provided a temporary respite, igniting their determination to continue the journey. In Cleveland, they discovered they would need to catch an accommodation train to Alliance to proceed further. However, heavy rainfall confined them to the waiting period in Alliance, preventing them from exploring the town. Nonetheless, their spirits remained high as they eagerly anticipated reuniting with loved ones.

Annie, writing in her diary, sent a telegram to her beloved husband,

Liv, requesting that he meet them at Rochester at 1 a.m. the following day. The rain continued to pour as the train resumed its journey, but Annie's impatience and curiosity grew with every passing mile. At Enon, Annie experienced a heartwarming surprise. "In walked Liv dripping wet," she wrote in her diary. Liv's unwavering love and dedication shone through as he braved the elements to greet his wife. The reunion of Annie and Liv brought sheer joy and relief, eclipsing the trials and tribulations of their travels. As Annie and Liv settled into their seats on the train, they cherished the shared experiences and adventures awaiting them in Pennsylvania. Annie's diary was a chronicle of their journey, revealing unexpected detours and tests of their resilience. Undeterred, they knew their path was leading them to a future filled with love, companionship, and remarkable adventures.

The echoes of Annie's diary entries resonated within the chapter, offering a glimpse into their journey and adding depth to their experiences. The quotes from the diary served as a testament to Annie's perspective and emotions throughout their travels, enriching the narrative of their remarkable adventure. As the train rumbled on, Annie's diary continued to captivate readers with heartfelt entries. The words penned on September 4th, 1875, echoed in Annie's mind, reminding her of the journey's significance. She reflected on the adventures they had encountered and those that lay ahead.

Annie recollected, filled with nostalgia, "Mary and I started for Pennsylvania. She is to spend a year with me." Her sister's presence brought comfort and reassurance. They embarked on the grand undertaking together, their bond growing stronger through shared experiences. Annie vividly remembered their arrival in rain-soaked Chicago. Seeking refuge at Alice George's residence on West Harrison Street, Annie smiled as she recalled Alice's hospitality. "She made us lie down and rest while she washed out, dried, and pressed our soiled skirts." This act of kindness affirmed their belief in the goodness of humanity.

The diary entries became a time capsule, capturing the essence of each moment. Annie's words transported them back to their exploration of Chicago, the visit to Lincoln Park, and the enchanting sights at the Exposition. The memories of the unique and intricate Eastlake-style rooms remained, leaving an indelible mark on Annie's artistic sensibilities. Their journey encountered challenges, including the train blunder that led them astray on a northern branch. Despite setbacks, they pressed on, fueled by their determination. Annie's diary chronicled their wait in Alliance, unable to explore the town due to heavy rainfall. Yet, their spirits remained unyielding as they eagerly awaited reunions.

Annie's telegram to Liv added anticipation to the narrative, signaling their imminent meeting. And at Enon, Liv's appearance, soaked from the rain, became a heartfelt surprise. Annie cherished his unwavering dedication, recounting how he had overcome hardships to be by her side. As the train chugged forward, carrying Annie and Liv closer to Pennsylvania, their hearts brimmed with excitement for their adventures. The quotes from Annie's diary had woven a thread of their journey, revealing trials, unexpected turns, and their unbreakable bond. It was a testament to their resilience and a reminder that their story was beginning.

Annie closed her diary, feeling a renewed sense of purpose and anticipation. Glancing at Liv, their hands entwined, they were ready to embrace the wonders of a new chapter in their lives. Guided by the "Through The Eyes Of Annie-Pages of the Past" and the promise of a future filled with love, companionship, and remarkable adventures, they eagerly embarked on the journey to Pennsylvania.

As the train rumbled along the tracks, Annie couldn't help but gaze out the window, captivated by the ever-changing scenery. The verdant green fields and rolling hills of the countryside passed by in a blur, each landscape more beautiful than the last. The rhythmic chugging of the locomotive echoed in her ears, a comforting backdrop to her thoughts.

Annie's mind wandered back to the day they had bid farewell to their family and familiar surroundings. The bittersweet moment was etched in her memory—the tearful hugs, the whispered words of encouragement, and the promises to stay in touch. Although they were embarking on a grand adventure, the pang of leaving loved ones behind lingered in her heart. Sitting beside her, Mary sensed Annie's contemplative mood and gently squeezed her hand. Their bond as sisters had always been strong, and this journey was a testament to their shared determination and spirit of adventure. Annie squeezed back, silently reassuring Mary that everything would be alright.

The train made a brief stop at a small station, and Annie took the opportunity to stretch her legs. She stepped onto the platform, breathing in the crisp air and absorbing the sights and sounds of the bustling station. Passengers hurriedly boarded and disembarked, their faces filled with anticipation and excitement. As the train resumed, Annie returned to her seat, her mind again drifting to her diary's pages. The quotes she had included served as milestones along their path, capturing the essence of each experience and emotion. They were fragments of her soul, preserved in ink, and they brought the story to life in vivid detail.

In her diary, Annie penned remarkable and mundane moments—the simple joys of a warm meal, a comfortable bed, and the company of kind strangers. These seemingly insignificant details were the threads that wove together the fabric of their journey, reminding Annie of the countless acts of kindness that had brightened their path.

As the train chugged onward, the landscape gradually shifted. They left behind the idyllic countryside and entered a bustling cityscape. The streets became narrower, the buildings taller, and the air filled with the hum of activity. Annie leaned closer to the window, eager to catch glimpses of the city they were approaching. Finally, the train came to a halt at their destination. Annie and Mary gathered their belongings, their excitement building with each passing moment. They stepped off the train, their eyes wide with wonder as they took in the sights and sounds of the new city. It was a place brimming with possibilities, where dreams could take flight and adventures awaited at every turn.

Hand in hand, Annie and Mary set off to explore the vibrant streets of Pennsylvania. The city embraced them, offering an assortment of cultures, flavors, and experiences. They meandered through bustling marketplaces, marveling at the array of goods on display. They wandered through quaint alleys, discovering hidden gems and stumbling upon charming cafes where they indulged in sweet treats and shared laughter.

With each passing day, Annie's diary grew thicker, its pages filled with the stories of their adventures. The quotes she had included remained constant reminders of their journey's significance, stirring her emotions and fueling her curiosity for the unknown that lay ahead. Annie and Mary were ready to embrace the wonders of their new chapter. They were two sisters bound by love and a shared yearning for discovery. With every step they took, they knew their journey would be etched in their hearts forever, a memorable chapter in the grand combination of their lives.

Chapter 11: Setting Up Home

Annie's long-awaited reunion with Liv in Rochester brought joy and a few unexpected mishaps. Upon our arrival, our excitement quickly turned to disappointment as we discovered that George, who was supposed to meet us, was nowhere to be found. Waiting for an hour felt like an eternity, and frustration started creeping in. We contemplated heading to a nearby hotel, but a familiar figure emerged in the distance just as we were about to give up. It was George, running towards us with relief and exhaustion written all over his face.

"Sorry for the delay," George gasped, trying to catch his breath. "I was waiting to see if Liv could work his magic and convince the conductor to make a stop near our home. But it didn't pan out, and I had to make my way back on a freight train. And to make matters worse, the seat in the carriage was broken, so I had to use the buckwagon instead."

Despite the unexpected setbacks and minor inconveniences, my excitement at finally being home was overwhelming. We reached our destination at three o'clock in the morning, and I could hardly contain my joy. After a much-needed restful sleep until ten o'clock, I woke up feeling refreshed and ready to dive into the next adventure: buying furniture for our new home. Thankfully, Liv could take some time off, and together, we set out for Sharon to fulfill this important task.

As Annie stood on the platform, scanning the faces of the bustling crowd, her heart fluttered with anticipation. The journey to Rochester had been fraught with excitement and anticipation, but now, faced with George's absence, a wave of disappointment threatened to dampen her spirits. She exchanged worried glances with Liv, silently sharing her apprehension about the unexpected events.

The time seemed to stretch endlessly as they waited for George's arrival, each passing minute amplifying their anxiety. Annie's mind raced with thoughts of what could have gone wrong, her imagination conjuring up scenarios of missed connections and unforeseen obstacles.

With every passing moment, The weight of uncertainty lingered in the air, casting a shadow over their reunion.

Just as they were on the verge of giving up hope, a familiar figure emerged from the crowd, sending relief through Annie's veins. It was George, his brow furrowed with exertion as he hurried towards them, breathless and apologetic. Annie couldn't help but feel a rush of gratitude toward him, knowing the lengths he had gone to make their reunion possible.

Annie was excitedly buzzing when they reached their destination in the early morning hours. The fatigue of their journey melted away as she stepped through the threshold of their new home, her heart brimming with anticipation for the adventures ahead. With Liv by her side and George's unwavering support, Annie knew that whatever challenges they faced, they would face them together, united in their shared dreams and aspirations.

Our journey to Sharon started in the evening, and we went to Liv's aunt Margaret Walker's house, where we would stay for the night. As we arrived, we were greeted by Aunt Margaret's husband, Mr. Walker, who was known for his peculiarities. At first, he seemed confused about Liv's name, questioning our identity. Thankfully, Aunt Margaret recognized the connection and clarified that Liv was Kittie Livingstone's son, Tom. With that confusion cleared, we were finally welcomed inside. Mr. Walker conversed with us for about an hour before retiring for the night.

The following day, Liv and I wasted no time and started our furniture shopping early. We spent the entire day exploring different stores, carefully selecting items to turn our house into a home. A light Brussels carpet for the parlor, an ingrain carpet for our room, and additional rugs were among the many things we purchased. We also acquired an extension table, a marble-top center table, and a bedroom furniture set. Blankets, counterpanes, tablecloths, and napkins were also on the list. But what surprised me the most was Liv's impulsive purchase of two large and striking oil paintings from an artist in New York. One depicted a breathtaking sunset on Long Island Sound off East Milford,

Connecticut, while the other captured a serene scene between Upper and Middle Haddam on the Connecticut River.

Returning home on Saturday evening, Liv and I embarked on the next phase of our journey: setting up our new home. We secured a dwelling in Mr. Garret's house on the corner of Broadway and Harmony Street. Though the house lacked remarkable visual appeal, the surroundings boasted magnificent elm and maple trees that provided shade. A spacious hall greeted us as we entered, with doors leading from Broadway and a side porch.

I took it upon myself to enhance the hall's appearance by adorning it with a beautiful red and green carpet and a bright Venetian border to expand its size. We borrowed a table from Mother K. and covered it with a red cloth to stand for the ice. Above the table, Liv hung the hat rack my father had given me above the table, adding a touch of sentimental value. With its grand old-fashioned mantelpiece and ample sunlight streaming in through the windows, the parlor quickly became a cozy and inviting space. A pale grey carpet adorned the floor, complemented by light paper featuring scarlet and gold borders. Gas lighting illuminated the room, with a pulley chandelier suspended in the center.

I meticulously arranged the furniture, placing the center table between the two front windows and adorning it with Albom vases. In the southwest corner, a small marble-top table held my way cross, a symbol of faith and protection. Two oversized green easy chairs, a pretty camp chair, and two elegant Austrian bentwood chairs completed the seating arrangements. Above the mantelpiece, we hung the Long Island picture, which the paper hanger had amusingly called the "waterscape." I placed my father's picture with a bracket and vase below between the south windows, a small tribute to his memory. Additional small artworks and ornaments adorned various nooks and corners, adding a personal touch to the room. A book rack filled with books and ornaments adorned one wall, while a drapery made of Southern Moss served as a backdrop, hanging across the door that led to Mrs. Garret's part of the house.

Brown shades trimmed with fringe and hanging baskets in the windows added a natural beauty to the room.

Moving on to the dining room, a small but cozy space, I covered the floor with a portion of the rag carpet made by my mother. We furnished the room with a walnut extension table and walnut chairs featuring perforated seats. A tiny cupboard housed my cherished selection of dishes, which we acquired at a more affordable price as they were considered seconds from the pottery in Beaver Falls. A white shade and a pretty white ruffled camberquire adorned the window, while a light paper with a small scarlet figure covered the walls. We added a round hanging bronze clock and several pictures to bring charm and cheer to the room.

The small kitchen had a window featuring a white shade, a rag carpet, a stove, a table, and a little cupboard for storing tinware. Uncle Matthew's generous gift of $50 furnished the dining room and kitchen, excluding the carpet.

Upstairs, I claimed a large room above the parlor as my personal space. The room boasted four windows, flooding it with natural light and creating a pleasant ambiance. Plain grey wallpaper adorned the walls, complemented by a blue and gold border. A grey carpet with a blue border covered the floor, providing a soft and cozy feel. The furniture, made of ash and walnut, included a marble-top bureau and washstand. Mats, cushions, and various blue-themed decorative items added the finishing touches. I found the room very pretty and inviting, a sanctuary where I could be myself.

The neighboring room above the hall became Mary's bedroom. It was a cozy space for her, with a small carpet featuring a bright pattern, a set of walnut chairs, and charming pink accents. A small room above the dining room also served as a storage area for trunks and clothes, providing much-needed organization in our new home. It would also be helpful if we decided to hire a live-in helper. With only one closet in the entire house, this small room offered valuable storage space.

With our new home now furnished and arranged, Liv and I embarked on the journey of married life, excited to begin this chapter together.

Our house was filled with our personal touch, reflecting our tastes and aspirations. It was where memories would be made, and dreams would come to life.

Chapter 12: Tea Parties and Visitors

After settling into their new home, Annie and Liv wasted no time making it their own. Liv's meticulous attention to detail ensured that the house met Annie's every expectation. "Liv has had a great deal of papering, painting, and fixing done to the house to please me, and it does please me," Annie wrote in her diary. She envisioned their home as a sanctuary of happiness and love.

However, despite the joy of their new home, Annie faced disapproval and hostility from Liv's mother and sisters. Their behavior deeply affected her, leaving her feeling miserable and isolated. "That I have been perfectly miserable for a week or more," Annie confided in her diary. She poured out her heart, seeking solace in her private thoughts. Recognizing the toll it took on Annie, Liv set up a separate home from his family, prioritizing his love and commitment to Annie above all else.

Once the house was in order and their spirits uplifted, Annie and Liv decided to host two tea parties to celebrate their new beginning. The first gathering was dedicated to the older family members, a testament to the enduring bond of kinship. "The first one for the old people," Annie noted in her diary. Their home welcomed Pa and Mother, Uncle Matthew and Aunt Isabella, Aunt Martha, Aunt Mary Kennedy, and Reverend and Mrs. Wallace. Annie noticed a troubling symptom in Aunt Isabella's right jaw and made a mental note to inquire about it and offer assistance.

The second tea party was a joyous affair, celebrating the younger members of the family and the union of Rob Kennedy and his bride, Anna Bonbright. "My second party was all the young folks of the family. Rob Kennedy and his bride Anna Bonbright, who were married on September 29th, 1875," Annie wrote in her diary. Cousins Sadie, Lorn, Will, Mary, Lizzie, and Sam, along with their own Sadie, George, and Anna, filled the house with laughter and merriment. Annie cherished these moments of togetherness, cherishing the bonds of family and the joy they brought.

Grandma Warner became the first visitor to stay with Annie and Liv in their new home. "My first visitor to stay was Grandma Warner. She came November 1st and spent several days with her, and she had a niece, Miss Tanner," Annie noted in her diary. The days were filled with stories and shared experiences, fostering a deeper connection between Annie and her grandmother. They embarked on a visit to the Pittsburgh Exposition, immersing themselves in the wonders of art and innovation. Annie stayed with Mary at Uncle Henry's until December 1st, 1875, savoring every moment spent with her loved ones.

During Annie's stay with Mary, she received a special visit from Miss Griselle, her Salem doctor, and her charming niece, Josie Taber. "While she was away, Miss Griselle, my Salem Doctor, visited me with her cute niece Josie Taber," Annie wrote in her diary. They marveled at Mr. Townsend's art gallery, which housed a collection worth $2500.00. This encounter deepened Annie's appreciation for the beauty of artistic expression.

On Thanksgiving Day, Annie's health worsened as she caught a cold and experienced a sickness. Confined to solitude, she found solace in Cousin Sadie and Aunt Martha's kindness and support. "Cousin Sadie and Aunt Martha were very kind to me," Annie expressed in her diary. Their comforting presence and loving care eased her discomfort, reminding her of the resilience and strength within her family.

As December approached, Annie's health improved, and she eagerly awaited Liv's return. Her spirits lifted when Mary, her dear sister, returned from her visit, bringing together Annie McClelland and her brother Rob. Together, they created new joy and companionship, further solidifying the family bonds.

As Annie continued documenting these events in her diary, she did so with renewed hope and optimism. "I hope we shall be delighted in it," she wrote, referring to their new home. She looked forward to the days ahead, believing that better times and happier memories awaited them. Their journey together, filled with love and resilience, was beginning.

Annie's heart swelled with anticipation as she imagined the joys and milestones that awaited them. She dreamed of holidays together, gathering around the dining table with seasonal decorations and sharing hearty meals prepared with love. The image of children's laughter echoing through the halls made her smile, and she eagerly anticipated the day their little ones would grace their home.

In her diary, Annie captured her aspirations for their life together. "May our home be a sanctuary of happiness and love," she wrote, envisioning a place where they could seek solace from the outside world and find comfort in each other's arms. She vowed to fill their days with affection, understanding, and unwavering support, building a foundation of love to withstand any challenges they might face.

As Annie poured her dreams onto the pages of her diary, she drew strength from the love that bound her and Liv together. Their unwavering commitment to one another was the driving force behind their journey, instilling in them the resilience to weather any storms that may come their way. They were determined to navigate life's uncertainties hand in hand, supporting and uplifting each other every step of the way.

With every word in her diary, Annie breathed life into her dreams. She believed that their new home would be the vessel that carried them through a lifetime of happiness and fulfillment. Their shared aspirations and unwavering love were the fuel that propelled them forward, forging a path that would lead them to a future brighter than they could ever imagine.

In the stillness of their new home, Annie found solace in her diary. It became a sacred space where she could express her deepest desires, fears, and triumphs. The diary bore witness to her journey, preserving their story for generations.

Annie's words echoed hope, optimism, and unwavering faith with every entry. She believed in the power of their love and the boundless possibilities that awaited them. Their journey was not merely about building a home but creating a life filled with love, joy, and shared dreams.

And so, with renewed hope and steadfast determination, Annie closed her diary, knowing their journey had only begun. She held onto the belief that their love would guide them through whatever challenges lay ahead and that their new home would be the backdrop to countless chapters of love, resilience, and cherished memories.

As the days passed, Annie found solace in the quiet moments spent within the walls of their new home; each morning brought a renewed sense of purpose as she embraced the routines of domestic life. From tending to the garden to preparing meals with care and precision, Annie poured her heart into every task, finding joy in the simple pleasures of homemaking.

With Liv by her side, Annie embarked on a journey of discovery, delving into the intricacies of married life and the bond they shared. Together, they navigated the highs and lows with unwavering determination, facing each challenge head-on and emerging more robustly.

Their home became a haven of warmth and hospitality, welcoming friends and family with open arms. Annie delighted in the laughter that filled the rooms, savoring the moments of camaraderie and connection that brought their home to life.

In the evenings, as they sat by the fire, Annie and Liv shared their hopes and dreams for the future, of shared aspirations. They spoke of the children they hoped to welcome into their home one day, imagining the sound of little footsteps echoing through the halls.

As the seasons changed, so too did their home, adorned with festive decorations and the aroma of holiday baking. Annie took pride in creating a welcoming atmosphere, infusing their home with the spirit of the season and the warmth of their love.

With each passing day, Annie grew more deeply in love with Liv, grateful for the life they were building together. Theirs was a partnership forged in love and strengthened by adversity, a bond that would withstand the test of time.

The future shimmered before them, filled with the promise of a life well-lived and a love that would endure. As Annie closed her diary, she embraced the certainty that their journey, rooted in love and fortified by their unwavering commitment, would lead them to a future brighter than their wildest dreams.

Chapter 13: Holiday Resilience and Renewal

When Mary returned home, she brought along Annie McClelland and her brother Rob, who stayed with them for a few days. Their presence added joy and liveliness to the household, and the days were filled with laughter and shared memories. Annie McClelland, Annie's cousin, was a spirited and energetic companion, while Rob's playful nature brought a sense of youthful energy to their gatherings. Together, they embarked on small adventures, exploring the nearby woods, picnicking by the river, and engaging in lively conversations that filled the air with joy.

"As Christmas approached, the anticipation of the festive season filled the McClelleland household," Annie wrote in her diary. "Annie's cousin Annie McClelland, accompanied by Aunt Eliza and another Aunt Livingston, arrived to celebrate the holidays together. The house became a bustling hub of activity, as the halls echoed with laughter and the aroma of seasonal delights wafted through the air."

However, the atmosphere was not entirely harmonious. Annie expressed her feelings in her diary, saying, "This crowded us considerably, and, as they were not very congenial spirits, things were not pleasant as they might have been while all were there." Despite the underlying tensions, the visiting aunts brought beautifully dressed young turkeys as gifts, showing their appreciation for the family gathering.

Annie prepared a magnificent feast for the upcoming New Year's dinner. "I roasted the largest turkey to perfection," she wrote proudly. The entire family gathered around the dining table, totaling ten people and themselves. "It filled the little dining room full, and I was just worn out with the work," Annie confessed in her diary. Nevertheless, she poured her heart and soul into the preparations, ensuring that every dish delighted the palate and reflected the warmth of their shared moments.

Amidst the joyful chaos, Annie harbored a secret, confiding in her diary, "Just about this time, I found out for a certainty that I had suspected for some weeks—that I was in a delicate condition." The news brought a mixture of emotions, ranging from joy to apprehension. She embraced this new chapter in her life with resilience and a determination to nurture her growing family and well-being.

As January arrived, the McClelleland house remained a hub of activity, bustling with visiting friends and relatives. Annie noted in her diary, "Mr. Bestwick was twice out, and Alexander's Hardware Store with several other buildings altogether, it just wore me out." Annie's diary entries revealed the toll the constant activity and responsibilities took on her physical and emotional well-being.

During this time, Annie also mentioned the health challenges faced by her loved ones. "After Annie left, I was very sick all through February 1876," she wrote. Mary, always a pillar of support, developed a painful carbuncle under her arm. Uncle Matthew Kennedy suffered intensely from a severe carbuncle on the back of his neck, causing concern for his recovery. Aunt Isabella continued to endure troubles with her face, causing both physical discomfort and emotional distress.

Annie's deteriorating health prompted Mary to plan to visit Mercer County, leaving Annie in need of additional assistance. Annie Maxwell, a young and inexperienced girl, was hired to provide much-needed help. "She came on March 7th, 1876," Annie noted in her diary. The presence of Annie Maxwell brought fresh energy and a welcome relief for Annie, allowing her to focus on her recovery and find solace in the support of those around her.

As the days gradually grew longer and the grip of winter loosened, Annie clung to the hope that spring would renew health and happiness. She embraced the changing season as a metaphor for her journey of resilience and rejuvenation. Through the diary, Annie's unwavering spirit persevered, intertwined with the threads of family, love, and the ever-present hope for a brighter future.

Annie Maxwell, a young girl eager to prove herself, quickly became indispensable to the McClelland household. She brought a fresh perspective and youthful enthusiasm, infusing the house with renewed energy. Annie took comfort in her presence, knowing she had someone to rely on during her moments of weakness.

Together, Annie and Annie Maxwell embarked on various projects around the house and in the garden. They planted vibrant flowers, their colors blooming in harmony with Annie's hopes for a lively and healthy future. Annie Maxwell's infectious laughter and optimistic outlook served as a balm for Annie's weary soul, reminding her of the joy that awaited her on the other side of her challenges.

As the winter months gradually gave way to the arrival of spring, Annie's health began to improve. She marveled at nature's rejuvenating power as the once-barren landscape transformed into a symphony of vibrant colors and sweet scents. Annie took solace in the beauty surrounding her, finding strength and inspiration in the natural world's resilience.

With each passing day, Annie grew more determined to embrace her role as a mother and create a nurturing environment for her growing family. She spent hours meticulously planning and preparing for the arrival of her child, ensuring that every detail was attended to with love and care. The anticipation of her baby in her arms filled her heart with profound joy and purpose.

Annie's unwavering spirit resonated through her interactions with those around her. She sought solace in the company of loved ones, cherishing the moments of laughter and shared memories that brought warmth to her days. Friends and family rallied around her, offering support and encouragement as she navigated the challenges of pregnancy and impending motherhood.

As the final pages of the diary filled, Annie believed that better times lay ahead. She cherished the moments of joy and laughter and shared memories that she had experienced. Each entry of hope and resilience left a lasting imprint on the pages of her life.

As the seasons changed and time moved forward, Annie's journey continued. The diary, a cherished companion, bore witness to her trials and triumphs, serving as a testament to the power of love, family, and the unwavering human spirit. It stood a testament to Annie's resilience and the steadfast love that guided her through even the darkest times.

As the winter months gradually gave way to spring, Annie's health improved, bringing a renewed sense of hope and vitality to the McClelleland household. With each passing day, she marveled at the rejuvenating power of nature as the once-barren landscape transformed into a symphony of vibrant colors and sweet scents. Annie found solace in the beauty surrounding her, drawing strength and inspiration from the natural world's resilience.

With the arrival of spring came a newfound energy and a sense of purpose for Annie. She spent hours tending to the garden, planting vibrant flowers whose colors bloomed harmoniously with her hopes for a lively and healthy future. The simple act of nurturing a new life filled her heart with joy and optimism, reaffirming her belief in the cycle of renewal and growth.

As Annie's health continued to improve, she found herself eagerly preparing for the arrival of her child, pouring her love and care into every aspect of their future together. She meticulously planned and organized, ensuring their home would be a sanctuary of love and warmth for their growing family. The anticipation of holding her baby in her arms filled her with a profound sense of purpose, driving her forward with unwavering determination.

Throughout this period, Annie found strength and support in the presence of Annie Maxwell, the young girl who had quickly become an indispensable part of their household. Together, they embarked on various projects around the house and in the garden, their efforts fueled by a shared sense of optimism and determination.

As the days grew longer and the grip of winter loosened, Annie felt renewed hope and optimism for the future. She embraced each day with gratitude and resilience, knowing that better times lay ahead for her and her growing family. The diary, a cherished companion throughout her journey, bore witness to her trials and triumphs, serving as a testament to the power of love, family, and the unwavering human spirit.

As she closed the diary for the last time, Annie couldn't help but reflect on the power of her own story. She had faced adversity head-on, turning her challenges into opportunities for growth and self-discovery. The diary had become a vessel for her hopes, dreams, and fears, capturing the essence of her remarkable journey.

In the following years, Annie's diary would be passed down through several generations, becoming a treasured heirloom of the McClelland family. Each reader would be inspired by Annie's resilience and unwavering spirit, finding solace in her words during their moments of struggle.

Annie McClelleland's legacy would live on, not only in the pages of her diary but also in the hearts of those who knew her and those who would come to know her through her words. Her story would remind us that even in the face of adversity, hope and resilience can guide us through the darkest times, leading us toward a brighter and more fulfilling future.

Chapter 14: A Visit to the Centennial Exhibition

In March, Annie and Liv received an invitation from the Fulton family to visit a place whose name was unknown. Rob shared his plans of going west soon, adding a sense of farewell to their preparations. As conversations about the upcoming Centennial Exhibition filled their household in April, Annie and Liv had to coordinate their schedules. Liv's availability only allowed him to join at the end of July, while Annie preferred not to go later than the first of June.

During this time, Dr. Griselle, Annie's doctor from Salem, informed her that she planned to attend the exhibition's opening. Encouraged by Liv, Annie decided to join Dr. Griselle and her mother on the trip. On May 8th, 1876, the journey began as Annie, Dr. Griselle, and her mother embarked on their adventure. They arrived in Philadelphia the following day, finding their boarding house on North 21st Street.

While Annie rested, Dr. Griselle and her mother explored the city's attractions, including the Masonic Temple and various art galleries. The anticipation built as the grand opening day of the Centennial Exhibition approached on May 10th, 1876. Mr. Gray, who had previously stayed at their house, joined Annie, Dr. Griselle, and the others as they made their way to the exhibition grounds.

However, their journey was not without challenges. Overcrowded streetcars and even a broken-down one caused delays and commotion. Undeterred, they gathered additional passengers willing to pay for a charter coach, determined to proceed with their plans.

As Annie and her companions navigated the bustling streets of Philadelphia, they found themselves enveloped in a whirlwind of sights, sounds, and sensations. The city's vibrant energy pulsed around them, fueling their excitement for the adventures ahead.

As the sun cast its golden rays each morning over the city, Annie and her fellow travelers explored Philadelphia's many attractions. From the grandeur of the Masonic Temple to the captivating art galleries that lined the streets, every corner of the city seemed to beckon them with promises of discovery and delight.

One particularly memorable moment came when Annie stumbled upon a small, tucked-away bookstore between two bustling thoroughfares. Enticed by the promise of literary treasures, she stepped inside, only to find herself transported to a world of wonder and imagination. Rows upon rows of books lined the shelves, their colorful spines whispering tales of far-off lands and grand adventures.

Lost in the labyrinth of literature, Annie whiled away the hours, her fingers tracing the spines of ancient tomes and modern classics alike. She lost herself in the pages of history, immersing herself in the stories of generations past and present.

However, not just the written word captivated Annie during her visit to Philadelphia. The city seemed to come alive with the exhibition's spirit, its streets teeming with vendors, performers, and curious onlookers from around the globe.

One evening, as the sun descended below the horizon and the city lights began to twinkle like stars in the night sky, Annie was drawn to the sounds of music and laughter emanating from a nearby square. Intrigued, she followed the sound until she stumbled upon a lively street festival, complete with dancers, musicians, and food vendors selling tantalizing treats from every corner of the world.

As Annie wove her way through the crowds of revelers, she couldn't help but marvel at the kaleidoscope of cultures and traditions on display. From the rhythmic beat of drums to the haunting melodies of European folk songs, the air was alive with the vibe of humanity.

At that moment, surrounded by the sights and sounds of the exhibition, Annie felt a profound sense of connection to the world around her. She realized that while the exhibition celebrated human achievement, it was also a testament to the power of unity and diversity.

And so, as Annie bid farewell to Philadelphia and returned home, she carried with her memories of grand exhibits and historical speeches and a deeper understanding of the world's beauty and complexity of the world in which she lived. It was a journey of discovery and enlightenment that would stay with her for the rest of her days.

As a Commissioner, Mr. Gray had access to the Grandstand and invited Annie to accompany him. The rest of the group searched for seats elsewhere but were unsuccessful. Among the sea of people, Annie recognized several acquaintances from Kansas, including Professor Henry Worral, Governor George Crawford, E.H. Bancroft of Emporia, and John Campbell of Fort Scott.

The Grandstand, opposite the Main Buildings, hosted the Thomas Orchestra and a chorus of one hundred singers in front of the art gallery. The opening ceremony began with a prayer by Bishop Simpson, followed by speeches from President Grant, Mayor Welsh, and General Hawley. Emperor Dom Pedro of Brazil and his wife were also present, although Annie only saw them. However, the event's highlight came with Myron Whiting's solo performance, which resonated through the vast crowd of 90,000 people.

After the official proceedings, a grand promenade through the buildings began, with the President and Emperor leading. President Grant initiated the operation of the immense Corliss Engine in Machinery Hall, a marvel that powered a significant portion of the machinery on display.

For dinner, Annie and her companions visited the restaurant of the South, managed by a Georgian who recreated the ambiance of the Southern style with Florida Moss and Palmetto trees. The afternoon was dedicated to exploring various buildings, with Annie feeling overwhelmed by the grandeur and abundance of things to see. She confessed in her diary that even if she had an entire book to fill with the names of what she saw that day, she would still struggle to convey a coherent understanding of everything.

Annie spent three weeks in Philadelphia, and during the second week, Mary joined her. Both found employment in the Kansas Department, utilizing their writing skills and earning a wage of $2.00 per day. However, as the days passed, Annie's homesickness grew, and Liv's loneliness became increasingly palpable. Eventually, Annie cut her stay short and returned home before Mary finished her exhibition duties.

The journey to the Centennial Exhibition was a significant chapter in Annie's life, filled with anticipation, adventures, and encounters with familiar faces. It marked a unique dimension of their time in Philadelphia, actively participating in the exhibition and contributing to the Kansas Department. The memories and experiences gained from this journey would forever be etched in Annie's diary, preserving the essence of that remarkable time in their lives.

As Annie wandered through the vast exhibition grounds, marveling at the grandeur and abundance of things to see, she couldn't help but appreciate the Centennial Exhibition's historical significance. It's been one hundred years since the signing of the Declaration of Independence, making it a momentous event for the entire nation.

The exhibition showcased the progress and achievements of various industries and nations, highlighting technological advancements, cultural displays, and artistic masterpieces. Annie found herself immersed in a world of wonders, from the impressive Machinery Hall with its colossal Corliss Engine powering the machinery to the creative displays in the Art Gallery and the captivating performances by the Thomas Orchestra and the chorus of one hundred singers. Beyond the sheer spectacle, Annie recognized the more profound significance of the Centennial Exhibition. It symbolized the progress and growth of the United States, showcasing the nation's industrial prowess, scientific innovations, and cultural diversity. It was a testament to the spirit of innovation and exploration that defined the era.

Annie's encounters with familiar faces from Kansas further emphasized the exhibition's importance as a gathering place for individuals from all walks of life. Meeting Professor Henry Worral, Governor George Crawford, and other acquaintances served as a reminder of their Kansas community and the shared aspirations for progress and prosperity. Participating in the Kansas Department added more significance to Annie's experience. By contributing her writing skills, she promoted her home state, showcasing its unique characteristics and achievements to the thousands of visitors attending the exhibition. It was a chance to celebrate and champion Kansas on a national stage.

In her diary, Annie chronicled the exhibits, speeches, grand promenade, and people she encountered. She captured the essence of the Centennial Exhibition, preserving its historical importance and impact on her life. For years to come, Annie would reflect on that remarkable journey and cherish the memories of when the nation came together to celebrate its achievements and envision a future filled with promise and possibility.

As Annie bid farewell to Philadelphia and returned home, she carried a sense of pride and awe for what she had witnessed. The Centennial Exhibition had not only provided an opportunity for Annie to immerse herself in the marvels of the time. Still, it had also deepened her appreciation for the historical significance of the nation's progress.

Back in Rochester, Annie reflected on the experiences she had gained while at the exhibition. The memories of the grand opening ceremony, the bustling exhibition halls, and the camaraderie shared with fellow Kansans lingered in her mind, each moment etched into her memory with vivid clarity. As she settled back into the routine of daily life, Annie often found herself leafing through the pages of her diary, reliving the sights and sounds of the exhibition. She marveled at the technological innovations in Machinery Hall, where the massive Corliss Engine symbolized America's industrial might.

The artistic displays in the Art Gallery had left a lasting impression on Annie, stirring her soul with their beauty and creativity. She was captivated by the intricate sculptures, vibrant paintings, and stunning works of craftsmanship adorned the exhibition halls. But perhaps most memorable were the encounters with familiar faces from Kansas. Meeting Professor Henry Worral, Governor George Crawford, and other acquaintances was a poignant reminder of Annie's roots and the strong sense of community that bound them together.

As Annie reflected on her time at the Centennial Exhibition, she couldn't help but feel a profound sense of gratitude for the opportunity to participate in such a historic event. It had been a journey of discovery and enlightenment, offering her a glimpse into her nation's progress and achievements. In the following weeks and months, Annie continued to cherish the memories of her time at the exhibition, drawing inspiration from the spirit of innovation and exploration that had permeated the air. She viewed the world through a new lens, filled with a renewed sense of wonder and curiosity.

The experiences gained at the Centennial Exhibition profoundly impacted Annie's outlook on life. They instilled in her a deep appreciation for the power of human ingenuity and the importance of celebrating progress and achievement. This journey enriched her soul and broadened her horizons, leaving an indelible mark on her heart.

As she penned her reflections in her diary, Annie knew that the memories of the Centennial Exhibition would stay with her for a lifetime, reminding her of the boundless possibilities that awaited those who dared to dream and explore. And as she looked towards the future, she did so with a renewed sense of hope and optimism, ready to embrace whatever adventures lay ahead. Annie wrote in her diary, "I reached home Saturday night and was in bed when Liv came home. He was not surprised when he lit the gas and found me there. We lay awake all night talking about the Centennial." The excitement and energy of their conversation permeated the air as they relived their experiences and shared their joys.

Chapter 15: A Surprise and a New Addition

Annie's homesickness and Liv's loneliness became overwhelming, prompting Annie to return home before Mary had finished her stay in Philadelphia. She arrived on a Saturday night, exhausted from the journey, and was already in bed when Liv returned home. His surprise was evident when he discovered Annie there, and they spent the entire night awake, talking about their experiences at the Centennial Exhibition. The familiar comfort of their shared stories and laughter filled the room, momentarily alleviating the ache of separation that had plagued them.

A week later, Mary returned home, and Annie took the opportunity to clear the house and prepare for their future endeavors. Throughout the summer, they engaged in abundant work, with Annie frequently preserving fruits and vegetables from their garden and hosting company. The McClelleland house became a hub of activity, with friends and neighbors gathering to share in the warmth of their hospitality. The aroma of freshly baked pies and jars of homemade preserves filled the air, creating an inviting atmosphere that brought people together.

On August 3rd, Mary began her journey home accompanied by Uncle Samuel Caldwell and Maggie Brown. The departure marked the end of a chapter, but it also signaled the beginning of a new phase for Annie and Liv. With the departure of their guests, the responsibilities of daily life resumed, and they took on their roles as caretakers of their homes. Annie found solace in tending to the garden, nurturing the vibrant flowers and vegetables that symbolized their hopes and dreams. On the other hand, Liv dedicated himself to maintaining their home, ensuring every corner was filled with warmth and love.

Amid their busy lives, Annie's brother Levi visited, sharing his intense desire for his wife to join Liv on his upcoming travels in October. Levi had been captivated by Annie's stories about the Centennial Exhibition and longed for his wife, Clara, to experience it. Annie and Liv warmly welcomed Levi, wishing to share their memories and excitement with a loved one. They engaged in lively discussions, carefully planning the logistics of Clara's journey and eagerly anticipating her arrival.

Annie noted in her diary, "Brother Levi was here on his way home from the Centennial. He was very anxious his wife should go with Liv when he should go in October, and she so arranged it." The bonds of family and the support they offered each other were evident in their discussions and decisions. Annie and Liv understood the significance of creating shared experiences and memories, and they were delighted by the prospect of Clara joining them on their future adventures.

As mid-August approached, Annie's mother planned to come and stay with her for a while. Annie saw an opportunity to fulfill her intuition that Liv should accompany Clara, Levi's wife, on her journey. She believed this would again allow Liv to visit the Centennial Exhibition and strengthen their family bonds. Annie wrote in her diary, "When Lou went home, he telegraphed to find out if Liv would not go with Clara the next week if she came on with her mother. I coaxed Liv to answer 'yes' - promising to behave myself while he was gone - only ten days. I felt something would prevent him from going in the fall if he did not go."

On August 24th, at 4 a.m., Annie's mother, Clara, and Clara's son Bert arrived. The house was excited as they prepared for their journey to the Centennial Exhibition. The anticipation of experiencing the wonders of the exhibition once more filled the air, infusing every moment with an electric energy. As the family gathered their belongings and bid farewell to their home, Annie couldn't help but feel a mixture of emotions—joy for the upcoming adventure and a touch of sadness at being temporarily separated from Liv.

Later that same evening, they embarked on their journey. The night was filled with a flurry of activity as they settled into the train, their spirits high with anticipation. It was a Wednesday, and the following Wednesday, August 30th, Annie organized a small party to mark the occasion. Friends and neighbors gathered at the McClelleland house, filling it with laughter, well wishes, and heartfelt excitement. Amidst the joyful chatter, a young man weighing several pounds and a half made his debut, capturing the attention and love of everyone present. The joyous occasion marked the arrival of a new addition to their family.

The family returned home on a bright Friday morning, and as Liv opened the front door, Annie's mother stepped out of the parlor, holding the baby in her arms. The room fell stunned as Liv's eyes locked onto the precious bundle. As time seemed to stand still, emotions welled up within him. He flew up to Annie and knelt beside her, showering her with kisses and tears of joy. The overwhelming happiness enveloped the room, leaving an indelible mark on their hearts, forever treasured as a symbol of love and newfound parenthood.

As Annie and Liv settled back into the rhythm of daily life, their home became a sanctuary of warmth and love, echoing with the laughter of friends and the gentle cooing of their newborn baby. Annie's return from Philadelphia brought a sense of completeness to their household as if alone could chase away the shadows of homesickness and loneliness that had lingered in their hearts.

In the quiet moments before dawn, when the world outside slumbered beneath a blanket of stars, Annie and Liv found solace in each other's arms. Their late-night conversations became a cherished ritual, a chance to relive the memories of their time apart and reaffirm the bond that bound them together. In those stolen moments of intimacy, they discovered a deeper understanding of each other, a shared resilience that grew stronger with each passing day.

As the weeks unfolded, Annie renewed her commitment to homemaking. Her days were filled with the simple joys of tending to her garden and preserving the bounty of nature's harvest. The kitchen became her domain, where she poured her love and creativity into every dish, transforming humble ingredients into culinary masterpieces that delighted the senses.

Meanwhile, Liv dedicated himself to the upkeep of their home, his hands skilled in carpentry and craftsmanship. With meticulous attention to detail, he restored worn furniture and repaired the creaking floorboards, infusing their home with a sense of warmth and stability that mirrored his steadfast presence.

Their days were punctuated by the arrival of friends and neighbors, drawn to the McClelleland house drawn by the irresistible aroma of freshly baked pies and the promise of lively conversation. In those moments of shared camaraderie, Annie and Liv found joy in the simple pleasures of human connection, their home becoming a beacon of hospitality and goodwill in their community.

As August gave way to September, Annie's brother Levi arrived, heralding the promise of new adventures on the horizon. Together, they eagerly discussed plans for Liv's upcoming travels in October, their excitement palpable as they envisioned the wonders that awaited them at the Centennial Exhibition.

Annie's diary entries offered a glimpse into the inner workings of her mind, capturing the hopes and fears that lay beneath the surface of their seemingly idyllic life. In her words, one could sense the longing for connection, the desire to create lasting memories with loved ones, and the quiet determination to overcome whatever obstacles stood in their way.

And so, as Annie closed her diary and tucked it away for safekeeping, she knew that their journey was far from over. The road ahead was uncertain, fraught with challenges and uncertainties, but she faced it with courage born of love and resilience. Together, Annie and Liv were ready to embrace whatever lay ahead, knowing that as long as they had each other, they could weather any storm that came their way.

The following week, as Mary returned home, Annie took the opportunity to clear the house and make preparations. She wrote, "Through the summer, did the greatest quantities of work. She put up fruit and had company nearly all the time." The bustling activity in their household mirrored the vibrant energy they had experienced during their time at the Centennial Exhibition.

On August 3rd, Mary began her journey home, accompanied by Uncle Samuel Caldwell and Maggie Brown. The departure marked the end of a chapter, but it also signaled the beginning of a new phase for Annie and Liv. The responsibilities of daily life resumed, and they embraced their roles as caretakers of their homes and families.

Amid their busy lives, Annie's brother Levi visited, sharing his intense desire for his wife to join Liv on his upcoming travels in October. Annie noted, "Brother Levi was here on his way home from the Centennial. He was very anxious his wife should go with Liv when he should go in October, and she so arranged it." The bonds of family and the support they offered each other were evident in their discussions and decisions.

As mid-August approached, Annie's mother planned to come and stay with her for a while. Annie saw an opportunity to fulfill her intuition that Liv should accompany Clara, Levi's wife, on her journey. She wrote in her diary, "When Lou went home, he telegraphed to find out if Liv would not go with Clara the next week if she came on with her mother. I coaxed Liv to answer 'yes' - promising to behave myself while he was gone - only ten days. I felt something would prevent him from going in the fall if he did not go."

On August 24th, at 4 a.m., Annie's mother, Clara, and Clara's son Bert arrived. The house bustled with excitement as they finalized their preparations for the journey to the Centennial Exhibition. The anticipation of revisiting the grand spectacle of innovation and culture consumed their thoughts. Despite the bittersweetness of parting with Liv briefly, Annie's heart swelled with pride and happiness for the adventure that awaited Clara and him.

With the arrival of their new addition, their family was complete. The love that radiated within their home was a testament to their journey, and Annie's diary entries reminded them of the remarkable moments they had shared.

As Annie closed her diary, she knew their story was far from over. The chapters of their lives would continue to unfold, filled with new adventures, challenges, and cherished memories. And together, Annie and Liv were ready to embrace whatever lay ahead, knowing their love would guide them through it all.

Chapter 16: Trials and Triumphs

After experiencing a prolonged and excruciating illness, Annie found herself bedridden for eleven agonizing weeks. She suffered from a debilitating condition called quinsy, a severe throat infection that caused intense pain and discomfort. The physical and emotional strain took a toll on her, leaving her feeling helpless and exhausted. And just as her health started to improve, another challenge presented itself—they had to dismantle their beloved home.

As the winter months settled in, casting a frosty veil over the landscape, Annie navigated the bitter cold with an added weight upon her shoulders. Her battle with quinsy had left her weakened and vulnerable, her body still reeling from the lingering effects of the illness. Each day felt like a marathon, with the simplest tasks becoming monumental challenges.

With Liv away and no hired help, Annie bore the full brunt of household responsibilities on her weary shoulders. The relentless demands of motherhood and the upkeep of their new home below Fallston Bridge left her feeling perpetually exhausted. From dawn till dusk, she toiled tirelessly, her days blending into a blur of endless chores and caretaking duties.

Their son's cries, Alfred, became the soundtrack of her days, a constant reminder of her unwavering commitment to motherhood. She tended to his needs with steadfast devotion, finding solace in the warmth of his embrace even amidst the chaos surrounding her. But as the nights grew longer and the exhaustion seeped into her bones, Annie longed for reprieve, for just a moment of respite from the ceaseless demands of her life.

On the rare occasions when Alfred slept soundly, Annie stole fleeting moments for herself, cherishing the quiet stillness of the night. With pen in hand, she poured her heart out onto the pages of her diary, finding solace in writing. Her diary became her confidante, a silent witness to her struggles and triumphs, a repository for her hopes and fears.

In her despair, Annie clung to the memories of happier times, drawing strength from the love she shared with Liv and their son. She found solace in the promise of brighter days, the hope of a future filled with joy and laughter. As she gazed into little Alfred's innocent eyes, she saw a reflection of her resilience, a reminder that there was always a glimmer of light, even in the darkest times.

But just as Annie began to glimpse the faint outlines of hope on the horizon, tragedy struck once more. On the day of their third anniversary, a shadow descended upon their home, casting a pall over what should have been a day of celebration and joy. Annie fell gravely ill, her weakened body unable to withstand the strain of hosting guests.

The arrival of cousins Ella and Belle Caldwell only added to Annie's burden, amplifying the weight of responsibility that already lay heavy upon her shoulders. Without the support of hired help, she felt as though she were drowning, the demands of her illness and her household threatening to engulf her.

From that fateful day in June until the first of November 1877, Annie's world became a prison of pain and despair. Half the time, she lay bedridden, her body too weak to move, while feeble attempts at activity marked the other half, her spirit crushed beneath the weight of her illness.

But amidst the darkness threatening to consume her, Annie found moments of fleeting joy. She clung to these moments like lifelines, tiny sparks of light in the suffocating darkness. As she chronicled her experiences in her diary, she found a semblance of peace, a glimmer of hope that whispered of brighter days to come.

Towards the end of November, when Annie was still recuperating, Mr. Gray and Minnie made a thoughtful stopover on their way back from the Centennial Exhibition. Annie's heart swelled with gratitude for their visit, as it provided a momentary respite from the dreariness of her illness. Her mother, who had been a constant source of support and comfort, had to bid farewell and return to her home. The separation was bittersweet, for Annie had relished the bliss of having her own home and managing the household for the past fourteen months.

Letting go was arduous, as it meant relinquishing a cherished sense of stability and independence.

As the autumn breeze carried a sense of anticipation, whispering promises of new beginnings and untold adventures, Annie longed for Liv's return. She yearned to share with him the past weeks' joys and struggles and revel in their boundless love for their son. With each passing day, she counted the moments until their reunion, imagining the stories they would share and the dreams they would weave together.

In the depths of her heart, Annie clung to the belief that their journey as a family was beginning, that the trials and tribulations they had faced were shaping them into stronger individuals and forging deeper bonds of love. And as she looked into the eyes of their little Alfred, she glimpsed a future filled with hope, laughter, and endless possibilities.

With every breath, she breathed in the essence of life, savoring the sweetness of each passing moment. The turning leaves painted a vibrant picture across the landscape, mirroring the changing seasons of their lives. And amid it all, Annie held tightly to the memories of that little party.

In the winter months, she brought moments of warmth and contentment despite the absence of their own home. Yet, Annie found herself shouldering an even more significant burden. With no hired help at hand, she bore the weight of motherhood, maintaining the household, and tending to the demanding needs of the baby. From changing diapers to washing clothes and undertaking all her ironing, Annie's days were consumed by endless tasks. The exhaustion settled deep within her bones, and she yearned for respite, a moment to catch her breath and rejuvenate her weary spirit.

On the first of March 1877, a glimmer of hope appeared as they moved into their new house below Fallston Bridge. The fresh start brought a renewed sense of anticipation and joy. Their precious son, Alfred Gray Kennedy, now six months old, was a hearty and lovely child, captivating their hearts with his infectious laughter and innocent charm. To Annie's relief, a capable and reliable maid joined their household, easing the weight on her shoulders. The days that followed were filled with moments of pure bliss as they reveled in the simple pleasures of family life and the comfort of a place they could call their own.

However, as the summer of 1877 approached, a dark cloud shadowed Annie's newfound happiness. On the day of their third anniversary, a celebration that should have been marked by joy and gratitude, Annie fell gravely ill. The strains of hosting a group of Good Templars from Philadelphia proved too much for her weakened body. The relentless demands of entertainment and her delicate health pushed Annie to her limits.

The following week, the arrival of cousins Ella and Belle Caldwell added to her already overwhelming workload. Without the support of hired help, the weight of responsibility threatened to crush her spirit. From that fateful day in June until the first of November 1877, Annie's world was confined to the confines of her bed.

Half the time, she was bedridden, unable to summon the strength to rise, while feeble attempts at activity marked the other half, her body too weak to accomplish even the simplest of tasks. It was a period of profound vulnerability and despair as Annie confronted the fragility of her mortality. The once vibrant and energetic woman was reduced to a mere shadow, grappling with uncertainty and its toll.

In those dark hours of weakness and pain, Annie's resilience was tested, and she confronted her mortality with a mixture of fear and acceptance. Yet, deep within her spirit, a flicker of hope remained. She chronicled her experiences in her diary, capturing her struggles and moments of fleeting joy.

"The folks came home Friday morning, and the mother stepped out of the parlor as Liv opened the front door, saying, 'Here is a present for you,' holding the baby out to him. Poor boy! He felt ready to drop, he said. He came flying up to me and knelt beside me, kissing me and crying over me in a way I can never forget."

Chapter 17: A Mother's Reflection

As Gray grew older, his personality blossomed into something truly captivating. He had a knack for being adorably mischievous and fascinatingly curious. Despite his best efforts, crawling eluded him, and his attempts often led him to move backward instead. Nevertheless, when he was nine months old, he showed remarkable determination and learned to stand independently, a feat he achieved shortly after donning his new short clothes in May 1877.

From an early age, Gray possessed a gift for gab. At four months old, he became a delightful chatterbox, filling the air with babbling, laughter, and self-conversations that could last for hours. It was a constant amusement and joy for Annie and Liv, who eagerly listened to his spirited expressions. During a three-week visit to Mr. McClelland's and Uncle Kenney's in Pittsburgh, they brought Gray along, and his delightful presence added an extra layer of happiness to their time spent away from home.

While dining at Mr. Miles' house one evening, Gray fondly occupied a big green chair called "The Dolly Cradle." His little hands were in constant motion, grabbing at objects with fervor, occasionally becoming noisy. Mrs. McClelland, amused by his antics, playfully remarked, "See here, young man, are you going to be a Methodist Preacher?" Gray paused and lectured to her with surprising seriousness as if comprehending her words. He then responded with a resolute "Ehuha," as if asserting his future intentions. The household erupted in laughter, enchanted by Gray's expressive nature.

In his baby babble, Gray often repeated the phrase, "Oh, Golly, golly, golly," with infectious enthusiasm. On a momentous day, Annie brought him home from an undisclosed location, and they decided it was time to baptize him. As Mr. Wallace poured water over Gray during the ceremony, the little one looked up, beamed with laughter, and uttered his endearing catchphrase, "Gully, gully, gully." The delightful spectacle brought smiles to all who witnessed it, leaving a lasting impression of Gray's playful spirit.

Capturing Gray's precious moments was a priority for Annie, and on the 22nd of May, when he was five months old, she arranged for his photographs to be taken in his adorable short clothes. One picture depicted him sitting and laughing, radiating pure joy, while the other showed him reclining as if playfully mimicking how he lowered himself down. The photographs captured Gray's ever-energetic and lively presence, preserving those cherished early memories for years to come.

June proved to be a month of adventure and challenges for Annie, especially as she navigated the responsibilities of caring for Gray without the assistance of a maid. One eventful workday, chaos ensued as Gray managed to find his way into the kitchen closet, causing a cascade of jars to tumble and spill beans across the floor. Meanwhile, the maid had discovered a leak in the tea kettle and placed it on the drain outside to be fixed later. Unbeknownst to Annie, he had slipped away while she was washing and dressing Gray and found himself sitting in the dirty drain, the tea kettle perched in his lap. Covered in grime, prompting Annie to quickly rescue him from the messy situation, cleaning and comforting him.

Despite the challenges, Annie's determination remained unwavering. She provided Gray with various playthings in the kitchen, but her respite was short-lived. Soon enough, she discovered Gray gleefully overturning a bucket of morning's milk onto himself in the pantry. Undeterred by the mess, Annie again tended to his needs, cleaning him up and offering him more toys to occupy his curious mind.

But Gray's exploration didn't stop there. On another occasion, Annie found him on the side porch with a bucket of nails that a worker had left there the previous day. With the cellar door slightly ajar, Gray amused himself by methodically dropping the nails, one by one, into the gap. To him, they seemed just as fascinating as any other object. Annie, realizing the ease with which he could wander off, kept a watchful eye to ensure he remained safely on the porch.

During a moment of respite, as Annie prepared dinner, she retrieved

Gray, only to discover him fast asleep. Exhausted and perspiring, his little hand still grasping a handful of nails, his flushed cheek rested against the door's incredible, sturdy iron ring. The sight of her sweet son, lost in slumber after a day of mischief, touched Annie's heart deeply.

In those precious and sometimes chaotic moments, Annie witnessed the marvels of Gray's growing personality and his insatiable thirst for exploration. Despite the challenges and occasional mischief, she treasured each experience, knowing that these small adventures shaped Gray's character and forged an unbreakable bond between mother and son.

As the days turned into weeks and weeks into months, Gray's development continued to surprise and delight Annie. His mischievous nature only grew more pronounced, and his curiosity seemed boundless. No object was safe from his little hands and curious mind. Annie often found herself chasing after him as he darted from room to room, exploring every nook and cranny of their home.

One particularly memorable incident occurred when Gray discovered the wonders of the backyard garden. Annie had spent hours tending to her flowers and vegetables, carefully nurturing each plant with love and dedication. But Gray, with his insatiable curiosity, saw the garden as a playground waiting to be explored. One sunny afternoon, as Annie turned her back for a moment to fetch a watering can, Gray seized the opportunity and ventured into the garden.

Annie's heart skipped a beat when she realized Gray was missing. Panic set in as she rushed outside, frantically searching for her adventurous son. And there he was, right in the middle of the garden, covered in dirt and with a mischievous grin. He had pulled up a handful of carrots, and his tiny fingers proudly clutched the vibrant orange vegetables. Annie couldn't help but laugh at the sight, admiring Gray's determination and resourcefulness.

But the adventure didn't end there. Gray's curiosity led him to discover the joy of mud puddles. After a rain shower, Annie watched in both amusement and exasperation as her son gleefully splashed and stomped in the muddy water. His clothes were drenched, and his face was adorned with dirt and pure bliss. Annie couldn't help but join in on the fun, setting aside her concerns about the mess and embracing the magic of childhood.

With each passing day, he brought new surprises and discoveries. Gray's vocabulary expanded, and his babbling became recognizable words and phrases. He loved mimicking the sounds he heard, whether birds chirping or their neighbor's dog barking. Annie marveled at his ability to absorb the world around him and make sense of it in his unique way.

Gray's magnetic personality drew people to him wherever he went. Strangers often stop and marvel at his adorable antics, struck by his infectious laughter and bright-eyed curiosity. Annie was proud to see her son bring joy to others, and she cherished the moments when their family was surrounded by laughter and love.

As Gray approached his first birthday, Annie couldn't help but reflect on the incredible journey they had embarked on together. Through the challenges and the joys, their bond had grown stronger. Gray had taught her the power of patience, resilience, and unconditional love. She knew their adventures were only beginning, and their lives would forever be intertwined in a beautiful shared experience.

As the days turned into weeks and weeks into months, Gray's development continued to surprise and delight Annie. His mischievous nature only grew more pronounced, and his curiosity seemed boundless. No object was safe from his little hands and curious mind. Annie often found herself chasing after him as he darted from room to room, exploring every nook and cranny of their home.

One particularly memorable incident occurred when Gray discovered the wonders of the backyard garden. Annie had spent hours tending to her flowers and vegetables, carefully nurturing each plant with love and dedication. But Gray, with his insatiable curiosity, saw the garden as a playground waiting to be explored. One sunny afternoon, as Annie turned her back for a moment to fetch a watering can, Gray seized the opportunity and ventured into the garden.

Annie's heart skipped a beat when she realized Gray was missing.

Panic set in as she rushed outside, frantically searching for her adventurous son. And there he was, right in the middle of the garden, covered in dirt and with a mischievous grin. He had pulled up a handful of carrots, and his tiny fingers proudly clutched the vibrant orange vegetables. Annie couldn't help but laugh at the sight, admiring Gray's determination and resourcefulness.

But the adventure didn't end there. Gray's curiosity led him to discover the joy of mud puddles. After a rain shower, Annie watched in both amusement and exasperation as her son gleefully splashed and stomped in the muddy water. His clothes were drenched, and his face was adorned with dirt and pure bliss. Annie couldn't help but join in on the fun, setting aside her concerns about the mess and embracing the magic of childhood.

With each passing day, he brought new surprises and discoveries. Gray's vocabulary expanded, and his babbling became recognizable words and phrases. He loved mimicking the sounds he heard, whether birds chirping or their neighbor's dog barking. Annie marveled at his ability to absorb the world around him and make sense of it in his unique way.

Gray's magnetic personality drew people to him wherever he went. Strangers often stop and marvel at his adorable antics, struck by his infectious laughter and bright-eyed curiosity. Annie was proud to see her son bring joy to others, and she cherished the moments when their family was surrounded by laughter and love.

And so, with a heart full of gratitude, Annie looked forward to the days ahead, eager to witness her beloved Gray's continued growth and development. She knew that no matter their challenges or how many mischievous escapades awaited them, their love would always be the guiding light that led them through the wondrous journey of motherhood and son hood.

Chapter 18: Milestones and Challenges

Dear little lamb, Gray was a source of constant joy and wonder as he reached new developmental milestones. Although Annie was restricted from lifting him due to her health, she found ways to ensure Gray could still enjoy the outdoors and the beauty of nature. That summer, she would let him sit in his buggy by the flowerbeds for hours, relishing in the sights and fragrances of the blooming flowers. As Gray delighted in the colorful petals, Annie sat beside him, engaging in play and cherishing their precious moments together. His tiny hands would flutter excitedly as he reached for the flowers, eagerly sniffing their fragrant essence. Annie would occasionally pluck a bloom, gently placing it in his mouth for him to explore, which always sent him into a state of pure delight.

As he grew older, Annie and Liv's daily routine with Gray became more intricate. With his increasing mobility and insatiable curiosity, keeping up with him became a delightful yet demanding task. Annie constantly adapted to Gray's evolving needs, ensuring that their home was a safe and stimulating environment for him to explore.

One sunny afternoon, Annie took Gray for a stroll in the nearby park, where they encountered a group of children playing with colorful kites. Gray's eyes lit up with wonder as he watched the kites soaring high above the treetops, their tails dancing in the breeze. Annie couldn't resist the urge to join in the fun, and together, they ran across the grass, chasing after the vibrant kites and laughing with sheer joy.

Moments like the one sent Annie and Liv about the simple pleasures in life, the moments of pure happiness and connection that made parenthood so fulfilling. They cherished every opportunity to share new experiences with Gray, knowing that each one was a precious memory in the making.

As Gray approached his first birthday, Annie and Liv began to reflect on the incredible journey they had embarked on together. They marveled at how quickly time had flown and how much their little boy had grown and changed in just one year. Gray's first birthday became a celebration of his milestones and their journey as a family.

Annie spared no effort in planning Gray's birthday party, inviting friends and family to join the festivities. The house was adorned with balloons and streamers, and a delicious cake decorated with colorful frosting sat proudly on the table. Gray's eyes widened with excitement as he took in the sight of the festivities, his infectious laughter filling the room.

It was a day filled with love, laughter, and cherished memories, a testament to Gray's joy in their lives. As Annie and Liv watched their son surrounded by loved ones, they felt overwhelming gratitude for the gift of parenthood and the privilege of watching their little boy grow and thrive.

Bath time was another cherished experience for Gray. He adored his bathtub and would kick and splash joyfully whenever immersed in the water. In the mornings, he would eagerly signal his desire to get out of bed, and Annie would lovingly wrap his little wrapper around him. Gray would then make his way around the bed, determined to reach the bathroom and his beloved tub, displaying his determination and independence even at such a tender age.

However, Gray's fondness for the tub waned. During Annie's illness, something frightened him, and he feared the tub afterward. It became a challenge to coax him back into the water, as he associated it with that distressing memory. Annie patiently worked to ease his fears, gradually reintroducing him to the joys of bath time.

One memorable Sabbath, when Gray was eleven months old, he let go of one side of the door and took his first unassisted steps across the room to the other side. It was a moment of pure pride and excitement for Annie and Liv, witnessing their little one venture into independent walking. In the afternoon, while revisiting Father K's, Gray let go of the door at the head of the basement stairs and walked along the hall to the foot of the stairs. His progress was astounding, a testament to his determination and growing confidence. However, the very next day, Gray fell ill, and his attempts at walking alone ceased until he reached the age of one. During those weeks of illness, Gray faced additional challenges with only two teeth, causing great concern for Annie and Liv. Seeking assistance, Annie brought him to Miss Griselle, who provided the necessary care to improve his condition. During his recovery, Gray's tiny mouth welcomed two more teeth, and in the fall, one more tooth emerged, albeit accompanied by discomfort. The poor little fellow cried through the night, but five new teeth had appeared by morning.

The journey of Gray's growth was not without its trials, but Annie and Liv faced each challenge with unwavering love and devotion. Together, they celebrated the big and small milestones that marked Gray's extraordinary journey of discovery and development.

During those weeks of Gray's illness, his tiny mouth, adorned with only two teeth, encountered additional difficulties. Annie and Liv anxiously sought assistance and turned to Miss Griselle, who provided the necessary care to improve Gray's condition. It was a trying time for the young family, but their love and devotion remained steadfast.

As Gray slowly regained his health, he began to overcome his setbacks. His growth journey was not without trials, but Annie and Liv faced each challenge with unwavering determination. Together, they celebrated every milestone, whether big or small, that marked Gray's extraordinary voyage of discovery and development.

Gray's bright smile greeted the world with even more teeth during his recovery. Two new teeth emerged, and in the fall, another tooth appeared, albeit accompanied by discomfort. The poor little fellow cried through the night, but by morning, the sun rose on a remarkable sight—five new teeth had sprouted, transforming Gray's once toothless grin into a charming display of pearly whites.

Annie and Liv marveled at their son's resilience and strength. They were reminded of the preciousness of life and the beauty of witnessing a child's growth. With every step Gray took, literally and figuratively, they cherished the moments and found solace in the knowledge that they guided him along this remarkable journey.

As the seasons changed, so did Gray's abilities and personality. His curious mind absorbed the wonders of the world around him, and his laughter echoed through their home, filling it with warmth and joy. Annie and Liv embraced the privilege of nurturing their son, relishing the pleasure of watching him grow and evolve.

The challenges they faced along the way only deepened their bond as a family. Each milestone became a testament to their unwavering love and devotion, a reminder that together, they could conquer any obstacle. And with every new tooth, every unsteady step, and every gleeful giggle, Annie and Liv felt a profound sense of gratitude for the privilege of being Gray's parents.

Their journey as a family continued to unfold, with each chapter revealing new adventures, lessons, and cherished memories. As they embarked on this remarkable voyage of parenthood, Annie and Liv held onto the promise of a future filled with endless possibilities and a love that would endure through all the trials and triumphs yet to come.

Chapter 19: Loss and Hope In A Missing Chapter

As Gray continued to grow, each passing day seemed to bring forth new milestones and unexpected challenges of joy and heartache that defined their journey as a family. Annie marveled at the wonders of motherhood, finding solace in the tender moments shared with her son yet grappling with the inevitable trials that tested her resolve.

One of the most memorable milestones came on a sunny afternoon in early September. Now a lively toddler of fifteen months, Gray took his first unsteady steps, reeling across the room with arms outstretched and a triumphant smile on his cherubic face. Annie and Liv watched with bated breath, their hearts swelling with pride at their son's new-found independence. They applauded his efforts, showering him with praise and encouragement as he wobbled from one end of the room to the other, determined to conquer the uncharted territory of walking.

But amidst the joy of Gray's achievements, there were moments of uncertainty and apprehension. As winter approached, Annie con-fronted the harsh reality of their circumstances. Liv's health, which had been a constant source of concern, showed signs of further deteriora-tion, leaving Annie to shoulder the responsibilities of caring for both her husband and their energetic son. The days stretched long and weary as she juggled the demands of household chores, tending to Liv's needs, and ensuring Gray received the love and attention he deserved.

Despite the challenges, Annie drew strength from the unwavering support of their community. Neighbors rallied around the young fam-ily, offering a helping hand and words of encouragement during their darkest hours. Whether it was a warm meal delivered to their doorstep or a reassuring hug shared in a moment of despair, these small gestures of kindness served as beacons of hope amidst the storm.

As the months wore on, Annie found herself grappling with con-flicting emotions. She cherished the fleeting moments of joy spent with Gray, reveling in his laughter and boundless energy, yet mourned the loss of the carefree days they once shared. The weight of responsibility pressed down upon her weary shoulders, threatening to engulf her in a sea of doubt and despair.

But through it all, Annie remained steadfast in her determination to provide her family with a nurturing and loving environment. She found solace in the simple pleasures of everyday life, finding joy in the sound of Gray's laughter and the warmth of Liv's embrace. Together, they weathered the storms that threatened to tear them apart, emerging more robust and resilient with each passing day.

As spring blossomed into summer, Annie reflected on the journey they had embarked upon together. The road ahead was uncertain and fraught with challenges, yet she faced the future with courage and optimism, knowing their love would guide them through even the darkest nights.

And so, as the sun set on another day, Annie held her son close, savoring the fleeting moments of peace and tranquility. She whispered words of love and reassurance, knowing that no matter what trials lay ahead, they would face them as a family, united in love and bound by the unbreakable bonds of kinship. As Annie turned the pages of her diary, she reached a point where her words abruptly ceased. The diary ended on page 70, leaving a void of unwritten memories. The following pages, 71 to 74, were torn out, forever shrouding their contents in mystery. However, the missing pages held crucial information to shed light on an essential event in Annie's life—the birth of her beloved son, Alfred Gray Kennedy.

The dates surrounding Alfred's birth were a subject of uncertainty and discrepancy. According to the available information, he was either born on August 30, 1876, in New Brighton, Beaver County, Pennsylvania, or on December 30, 1876, in Beaver, Beaver County, Pennsylvania. In her diligent research, Annie concluded that her pregnancy began in January 1876, as pregnancies typically span nine months. This led her to believe that Alfred's actual birth date was closer to August 30, 1876, contradicting the previously assumed December date.

The importance of clarifying Alfred's birth date was tragically underscored by his untimely death in May 1879. Newspaper clippings from that devastating time reported that Alfred was only two years, eight months, and two days old when he passed away. The weight of this loss weighed heavily on Annie's heart, forever etching the memory of her cherished son in her diary.

Though the exact details of Alfred's early years and the experiences captured within the missing pages of Annie's diary remain unknown, their absence speaks volumes. The torn-out pages symbolize the gaps in our understanding of the past, reminding us that history, like life itself, is often marked by unanswered questions and elusive fragments.

While the missing chapter remains a source of curiosity and longing, Annie's unwavering love for her son endures. She may not have penned the details of those specific years, but her heart carried the memories of Alfred's birth, his laughter, his growth, and the overwhelming sorrow of his loss due to the dreaded disease, diphtheria.

In the quiet moments of reflection, Annie found solace in her profound bond with her beloved Alfred. Though incomplete, their story is a testament to the enduring power of a mother's love and the profound impact a precious life can have in the briefest moments. Alfred Gray Kennedy's presence, however fleeting, left an indelible mark on Annie's heart and the pages of her life. As Annie grappled with the devastating loss of her firstborn son, she found solace in the bittersweet moments of her pregnancy with the twin boys growing within her. The weight of grief intertwined with the anticipation of new life, creating a uniqueness of emotions that both challenged and uplifted her spirit.

At seven months pregnant, Annie's belly swelled with the promise of new beginnings. The kicks and flutters of her unborn twins served as gentle reminders that life, in all its complexities, continued to weave its intricate threads. A glimmer of hope flickered in the darkness of sorrow, reminding Annie of the precious gift she carried within. With the sorrow of her loss, Annie experienced a range of emotions. There were moments when grief threatened to consume her entirely, leaving her feeling adrift in an ocean of sadness. Yet, there were also moments of joy and gratitude as she marveled at the miracle unfolding within her. The delicate balance between grief and happiness became a tight-rope Annie walked, never knowing which emotion would tip the scales on any given day.

Annie sought refuge in the support of her loved ones, leaning on Liv's unwavering presence and finding solace in the understanding of family and friends. Their love surrounded her, creating a haven where she could navigate the complexities of her emotions.

As the months progressed, Annie's anticipation grew, mingling with trepidation. The impending arrival of her twin boys was a beacon of light amid her grief, but it also brought a twinge of anxiety. Would she be able to fully embrace the joy of their birth while still mourning the loss of her firstborn? It was a question that weighed heavily on her heart. Yet, as the days counted to July, Annie discovered a newfound strength within herself. She realized that her love for her firstborn and her passion for her unborn twins was not mutually exclusive. She could honor the memory of her lost son while embracing the joy of the new lives blossoming within her.

In the quiet moments, as she placed her hands on her growing belly, Annie felt a profound connection to her babies. She whispered words of love and resilience, promising them a world filled with hope and determination. They became her guiding light, reminding her that life was full of loss and happiness and that strength could be found in their delicate balance. With each passing day, Annie's heart swelled with love and longing. The journey she was embarking upon was one of profound complexity, where grief and joy intertwined like the ivy on an ancient tree. As she prepared to welcome her twin boys into the world, Annie knew their arrival would bring healing for her and the entire family.

The anticipation of their birth became a beacon of hope, a reminder that life was a fabric in motion, where the threads of loss and happiness were intricately woven together. Annie's journey through grief and the anticipation of new life became a testament to the resilience of the human spirit and the power of love to transcend even the darkest moments. As the days turned into weeks and the weeks into months, Annie's heart grew with anticipation, ready to embrace the joys and challenges ahead. The birth of her twin boys would mark the beginning of a new chapter in her life, one that would forever be intertwined with the memory of her firstborn son.

In the face of loss, Annie found the courage to embrace the happiness that awaited her, knowing that her love for her children would continue to grow and evolve, transcending the boundaries of time and space. As she awaited the arrival of her twin boys, Annie held onto the belief that even in the face of darkness, there was always the promise of light.

Chapter 20: The Dawn of Destiny

The question lingered in the air, whispered among the guests and hidden within Annie's heart—how did Thomas Livingston Kennedy and Annie Wadren Caldwell come to be? Annie discovered a familial link between Thomas's mother, Catherine P. Livingston Kennedy, and Annie's own kin. Catherine had a sister named Eliza Jane Livingston Caldwell, who married Samuel Caldwell II—a brother to Annie's father, William Caldwell. The revelation unveiled a web of connections, with Thomas and Annie being first cousins.

Growing up, Thomas would have watched Annie blossom into a young woman. Their families, residing within an hour's distance of each other in Pennsylvania, would often gather, allowing the two to interact. Holidays and special occasions provided ample opportunities for Thomas to witness Annie's growth, while his mother Catherine cherished the moments spent with her sister Eliza Jane.

Although adulthood brought geographical separation, with William Caldwell living in Illinois and Samuel Caldwell in Pennsylvania, the ties of kinship remained. William, who had been raised in Mercer County, Pennsylvania, had ventured to Illinois after the passing of his first wife, Sarah Lindsey. It was there that he remarried Rosina Menold, Annie's mother. William's mother, Elizabeth Donaldson Caldwell, passed away in June 1870, prompting a reunion of the Caldwell brothers.

During this somber time, Annie, now 18 years old, stood beside her sister Eliza and brother-in-law Samuel as they mourned the loss of their beloved grandmother. It was there, the grieving, that she caught a glimpse of Thomas Livingston Kennedy once again—a 28-year-old man, standing alongside his mother Catherine. The connection once seeded in their childhood encounters began to flourish anew.

Annie's attendance at her grandmother's funeral marked a turning point in their relationship. The shared sorrow provided a backdrop for rekindled emotions and unspoken connections. In the face of loss, they found solace in each other's presence, their shared history intertwining with their shared future.

From that moment onward, Annie and Thomas embarked on a courtship that transcended distance and circumstance. Their love blossomed, nurtured by the echoes of their familial ties and the memories forged in the crucible of shared experiences.

And so, on this fateful day in June 1874, Annie stood poised to embark on a new chapter of her life—a union foretold by the threads of family and destiny. As the clock struck nine, she took her place beside Thomas, ready to forge a path together. The winds of change continued to blow, but now, they carried whispers of promise and happiness, gently guiding Annie Wadren Caldwell and Thomas Livingston Kennedy into the embrace of their shared future.

As Annie and Thomas entered into the realm of matrimony, their love story became a beacon of hope and inspiration for those around them. Their courtship was not without its challenges, as distance and circumstance often conspired to keep them apart. Yet, their unwavering commitment and deep-rooted connection propelled them forward.